"I cannot think of another book on making peace with the earth that does so much in so few pages—grounding its case with theological care, describing the causes of 'ecological amnesia' so clearly that they are impossible to disown and offering a vision of practical response that appeals to hope instead of guilt, and all of this while telling stories that make the book difficult to put down! Here is a book for anyone who is ready to trade ecological despair for practical action, in the company of two men who know what it means to be 'married to the land.'"

BARBARA BROWN TAYLOR, author of *An Altar in the World*

"Bahnson and Wirzba have written a compelling summons to food repentance. They call us away from the long-term unsustainable bubble of food in the orbit of fossil fuel. They urge return to the quotidian reality of soil, fresh tomatoes, the daily work of gardening and realism about the source of food. Their accessible, anecdotal style adds force to the critical bite of their invitation toward life-giving, life-sustaining food."

WALTER BRUEGGEMANN, Columbia Theological Seminary

"*Making Peace with the Land* offers a powerful vision of God as a gardener, physically engaged in the work of restoring all creation to wholeness. And it offers hungry people a way to join in God's work by getting our hands dirty. This is a book about communion in its deepest sense."

SARA MILES, founder of The Food Pantry and author of *Take This Bread: A Radical Conversion*

"This series is on reconciliation, which is at the heart of the Christian faith. One of the early Christians said there are three dimensions to the cross—the vertical, which is about reconciliation with God; the horizontal, which is about reconciliation to other humans; and finally the cross is firmly planted into the earth, which calls us to reconcile with creation. That final dimension is perhaps the most neglected one of all in the piles of books on faith. I am deeply thankful for this addition to the library. We all just got smarter."

SHANE CLAIBORNE, author, activist and recovering sinner, www.thesimpleway .org

"When Mary turned from the empty tomb and mistook Jesus for a gardener, it was no mistake: Jesus is the new Adam. Thank you, Fred and Norman, for reminding us of our Genesis 2:15 responsibility to tend and protect the Garden, this earth, and calling each of us to the good work of living peaceably with the land."

NANCY SLEETH, cofounder, Blessed Earth, and author of *Almost Amish*

MAKING PEACE WITH THE LAND

God's Call to Reconcile with Creation

FRED BAHNSON
& NORMAN WIRZBA

Foreword by BILL MCKIBBEN

Resources for Reconciliation

Series editors

EMMANUEL KATONGOLE & CHRIS RICE

IVP Books

An imprint of InterVarsity Press
Downers Grove, Illinois

InterVarsity Press
P.O. Box 1400, Downers Grove, IL 60515-1426
World Wide Web: www.ivpress.com
E-mail: email@ivpress.com

InterVarsity Press® is the book-publishing division of InterVarsity Christian Fellowship/USA®, a movement of students and faculty active on campus at hundreds of universities, colleges and schools of nursing in the United States of America, and a member movement of the International Fellowship of Evangelical Students. For information about local and regional activities, write Public Relations Dept., InterVarsity Christian Fellowship/USA, 6400 Schroeder Rd., P.O. Box 7895, Madison, WI 53707-7895, or visit the IVCF website at <www.intervarsity.org>.

Scripture quotations, unless otherwise noted, are from the New Revised Standard Version of the Bible, copyright 1989 by the Division of Christian Education of the National Council of the Churches of Christ in the USA. Used by permission. All rights reserved.

While all stories in this book are true, some names and identifying information in this book have been changed to protect the privacy of the individuals involved.

Cover design: Cindy Kiple
Images: Fellowship outside and around the table by Rick Beerhorst

ISBN 978-0-8308-3457-0

Printed in the United States of America ∞

Library of Congress Cataloging-in-Publication Data

Bahnson, Fred, 1973-
 Making peace with the land: God's call to reconcile with creation/
Fred Bahnson and Norman Wirzba.
  p. cm.——(Resources for reconciliation)
 Includes bibliographical references (p.   ).
 ISBN 978-0-8308-3457-0 (pbk.: alk. paper)
 1. Human ecology——Religious aspects——Christianity. 2. Ecotheology.
3. Reconciliation——Religious aspects——Christianity. I. Wirzba,
Norman. II. Title.
  BT695.5.B34 2012
  261.8'8——dc23

2012000263

P	17	16	15	14	13	12	11	10	9	8	7	6	5	4	3	2	1
Y	26	25	24	23	22	21	20	19	18	17	16	15	14	13	12		

FRED:

For my mother, who taught me to love words,

and for my father, who taught me to love the land.

NORMAN:

For my children Emily, Anna, Benjamin and Luke

Contents

Series Preface

The Resources for Reconciliation Book Series

A partnership between InterVarsity Press and the Center for Reconciliation at Duke Divinity School, Resources for Reconciliation books address what it means to pursue hope in areas of brokenness, including the family, the city, the poor, the disabled, racial and ethnic divisions, violent conflicts, and the environment. The series seeks to offer a fresh and distinctive vision for reconciliation as God's mission and a journey toward God's new creation in Christ. Each book is authored by two leading voices, one in the field of practice or grassroots experience, the other from the academy. Each book is grounded in the biblical story, engages stories and places of pain and hope, and seeks to help readers to live faithfully—a rich mix of theology, context and practice.

This book series was born out of the mission of the Duke

Divinity School Center for Reconciliation: Advancing God's mission of reconciliation in a divided world by cultivating new leaders, communicating wisdom and hope, and connecting in partnership to strengthen leadership. A divided world needs people with the vision, spiritual maturity and daily skills integral to the journey of reconciliation. The church needs fresh resources—a mix of biblical vision, social skills of social and historical analysis, and practical gifts of spirituality and social leadership—in order to pursue reconciliation in real places, from congregations to communities.

The ministry of reconciliation is not reserved for experts. It is the core of God's mission and an everyday call of the Christian life. These books are written to equip and stimulate God's people to be more faithful ambassadors of reconciliation in a fractured world.

For more information, email the Duke Divinity School Center for Reconciliation at reconciliation@div.duke.edu, or visit our website: <http://dukereconciliation.com>.

Emmanuel Katongole
Chris Rice
Center codirectors and series editors

Foreword

*W*hy are we surprised when we find the Bible addressing, in the most straightforward terms, the problems we face?

Ever since Lynn White's famous essay in the late 1960s, people have been happy to blame the Genesis worldview for many of our environmental troubles. We were granted "dominion" over the planet and used that as license to wreck it, or so the theory goes. And given the largely wrecked planet, and the Christian heritage of the biggest wreckers, it was a reasonable thesis.

But of course no one consciously set out to destroy the earth, and most of the time no one had much idea that that was what they were doing. It's only in the last few decades that we've begun to understand the extent of the damage—and it's precisely in that period that we've seen the accelerating rise of a religious environmental movement, something this book both reflects and will help spur.

The most important part of that movement is the dawning understanding that God cares about the earth. This only strikes us as revelation because we didn't need to pay attention to it for several millennia. The real dramas for most of the Christian era have been between people: war, injustice, bigotry. So we naturally read the Bible for advice on those questions. The Exodus story became the backdrop of the civil rights movement, and so on.

But now that the drama has turned to the suddenly fraught relationship between people and the rest of creation, it hasn't taken long to figure out Scripture is filled with resources that can help us here too. In fact, you don't need to go very far. The very first page of the Bible is an account of God building a beautiful world and giving us, yes, dominion over it. Putting us in charge. It turns out this is, in our moment, an entirely accurate depiction: as we've changed the atmosphere by pouring carbon into the air, we've taken control of every square inch of the earth. We increasingly determine the temperature, and with it the evaporation, the precipitation, the change of seasons. And we come to understand the real meaning of dominion: to do a responsible, good job, not a lousy one. If you leave your kids with a babysitter, you'd be dismayed to come home and find them with tattoos and pierced noses. I imagine God feels somewhat the same.

In any event, this book reminds us of the resources—scriptural, scientific and human—that we have as we try to write a new story, one that emphasizes the need for people to back off, to allow the planet to operate on its own (God's) terms instead of ours. It's a rich book, which is appropriate, since this is a rich and beautiful world.

Bill McKibben
Founder, 350.org
Schumann Distinguished Scholar,
Middlebury College, Vermont

Prologue

For God So Loved the Soil . . .

And the Lord God planted a garden in Eden.

Genesis 2:8

*H*ow many sermons have you heard that describe God as a gardener, with knees on the ground and hands in the dirt? God the *Gardener*?

First impressions matter, making it all the more striking that this is exactly how Scripture first presents God. God does not create the world from a lofty and disinterested height or through means of violent force. Instead, God enlists and then engages the soil so that the earth puts forth all kinds of vegetation and fruit and "bring[s] forth living creatures of every kind" (see Gen 1:11-13, 24). God is committed to the soil from the beginning, because it is *through* the ground that the great variety and fertility of life come to blossom. No wonder that God loves the soil.

In Genesis 2, the centrality of soil is even more pronounced than in Genesis 1. Here God fashions the first human being by taking the dust of the ground into his hands, holding it so close that it can share in the divine breath and inspiring it with the freshness of life. It is only as the ground is suffused with God's intimate, breathing presence that human life—along with the life of trees and animals and birds—is possible at all (see Gen 2:9, 19). God draws near to the earth and then animates it *from within*.

We are right to believe that God loves you and me. But in these earliest pages of Scripture, we discover that God's first love is the soil. This is how it has to be, because without healthy soil and the fertility and food it makes possible, there would be no terrestrial life of any kind. God's love for us—described definitively in John 3:16 as God's giving of his Son to us—only makes sense in terms of God's love for the earth that sustains us. God daily cares for us by providing the nurture of food, as well as the gifts of fiber and timber and energy, all of which find their origin in soil.

Only as we grasp God's love for the earth can we begin to feel God's regret as recorded in Genesis 6:6-7: "And the LORD was sorry that he had made humankind on the earth, and it grieved him to his heart. So the LORD said, 'I will blot out from the earth the human beings I have created—people together with animals and creeping things and birds of the air, for I am sorry that I have made them.'" Human disobedience, arrogance and violence—to which the soil constantly bears witness—had so degraded and destroyed creation's order and beauty that God resolved to wipe it out with a deluge of rain and mud. What began as a garden of "delight" (which is what *Eden* really means) quickly became a nightmare of drowning and death.

The nightmare is not over. God promised to never again destroy the world, but we humans just might. The findings of ecologists and environmental historians show that people have yet to learn what is required to live harmoniously on and with the earth. God's soil and water are daily being poisoned and wasted. God's forests and glaciers are quickly disappearing. God's animals, particularly the agricultural animals that we have domesticated, are systematically being abused. And perhaps worst of all, we are causing the "dome in the midst of the waters," that protective mantle we call the *atmosphere*, to rupture (Gen 1:6). Polar ice is melting, hurricanes and droughts are becoming more frequent and severe, sea levels are rising, and the tropics have expanded by two degrees latitude. All of these things will make life here much more precarious in the coming decades, especially for the world's poor. Genuine human flourishing depends upon the health of the land and its creatures.

God has a different vision for us, a vision in which people live in reconciled rather than exploitive relationships with creation. God takes the first human being (*adam*) freshly formed from the soil (*adamah*), and says, *Take care of the garden. Learn to serve and protect the ground. Commit to loving the soil, and in this loving work catch a glimpse of who I am and what I do.* That

God "took the man and put him in the garden of Eden to till it and keep it" (Gen 2:15) is an invitation to know and share in God's love for the whole creation. It is a summons to join in the hard, divine work that, by nurturing soil, nurtures human life. From the beginning and forever, God's life is a sustained act of caring for the earth and its many creatures, breathing into the world whatever life we behold. How did we come to think that participating in God's care of the world is an unworthy or demeaning calling?

We need to learn again how to live in the garden: not the Eden we've lost, but the garden of the New Jerusalem toward which we're bound. When we garden well, we do not only grow food for our bodies and flowers for our tables; we share in and extend God's feeding, healing and sustaining ways with the world. With more honesty and practical discipline than our words can convey, we demonstrate an appreciation for the divine love that forever cherishes the earth.

God is the first, the best and the most essential Gardener. God's gardening work is the most fundamental and indispensable expression of the divine love that creates, sustains and reconciles the world. This love is not abstract. Nor is it vaguely spiritual. It is a love that brings us down to our knees so that we can immerse our hands in the soil. There is no more basic or humble or noble calling than participating in God's love for the earth.

I

Reconciliation with the Land

NORMAN WIRZBA

*I*n the fall of 1986, I left the foothills and plains of southern Alberta to begin a master's degree at Yale Divinity School. On my way, I traveled through Gary, Indiana. Nothing prepared me for what I experienced there: thick gray air, an unbelievably foul smell, a greenish-orange cloud in place of the horizon and smokestacks belching putrid poison into the sky.

I couldn't believe people lived there. I saw a few men fishing in lagoons of brackish, foamy water. What sort of fish could possibly be living in this sludge? I wondered if they ate what they caught. What kind of health issues did these men and their families face, surrounded as they were by toxic water, land and air? Knowing it was a futile gesture, I opened my window and yelled to the world outside.

It took me a long time to absorb what I saw. I'm still absorbing it. The air that I knew as a farm boy in southern Alberta was crisp and clear and even fragrant, often carrying the scent of sweet grass. The Rocky Mountain snowpacks an hour to my west provided clean, fresh water. And the deep brown soil smelled of fertility. The contrast with Gary was jarring.

I know it is dangerous to put too much stock in childhood memories. Was I being naive in remembering only the good and pleasant parts? As children, we don't have the complicated understanding we gradually acquire as adults, and I now recognize that plenty of problems were associated with the industrial agriculture and resource development taking hold in Alberta. Still, as I drove through Gary, I knew with the certainty of my nose and eyes that something was deeply wrong with the way this section of the Great Lakes region, with its plant and animal and human inhabitants, was being treated.

When I arrived at Yale, I discovered that almost no one was talking in theological terms about our capacity to destroy the land. The stench and death that Gary exhibited hardly appeared as a theological concern or problem. Although almost everyone I met professed belief in God as the Creator—indeed, this may be one teaching that most people professing belief in God can agree on!—it seemed that creation itself was of little concern. Surely it is a contradiction to profess belief in the Creator while showing disregard or disdain for the works of the Creator's hands.

THE WIDE SCOPE OF GOD'S
RECONCILING CONCERNS

Today's church suffers from a reconciliation deficit disorder. The cause of this disorder is an impoverished imagination. As Christians, we have a hard time imagining that God desires all creatures—human and nonhuman, living and nonliving—to be reconciled with each other and with God. For a variety of reasons, we have come to think that God cares primarily, perhaps only, about us.

The history of the church shows that Christians have frequently curtailed the scope of what and whom God cares about. Are we to include everyone—all men and women and children, all races and ethnic groups, all social and economic classes—within the group that God chooses to love and save? Should we think of God's salvific purposes as including bodies, communities and the land? Maybe God cares only about individual souls (white, male, American, heterosexual, economically successful) making their way to heaven.

Clarence Jordan, founder of Koinonia Farm in Americus, Georgia, said that as a child of the Jim Crow South he sang, "Jesus loves the little children, all the children of the world. Red and yellow, black and white, they are precious in his sight. Jesus loves the little children of the world." He sang this, Jordan recalled as an adult, while watching the poor, hungry black children of his town be mistreated by the members of his congregation. Could it be that God had favorite children, or was it that *we* were picking favorites? Jordan was seeing the propensity of humans to limit the scope of God's love. Depending on your class, race and even gender, you were either *in* the group God really cared about or *out* of it. As Jordan later turned the wasted and abused red clay of southwest Georgia into a productive farm and forest, he must have wondered if we as a species had also come to limit God's love only to humanity, thus forgetting God's love for the whole creation.

As members of the early church thought about the significance of Christ's life and ministry, they came to an astounding affirmation of the cosmic, all-inclusive scope of God's love. The long arc of God's redemptive purposes is not confined to individual, disembodied souls, let alone souls of a particular gender or race or ethnicity or class. Referring to Jesus, they sang in one of their earliest hymns that "all things in heaven and on earth," "things visible and invisible," were created *in* him, *through* him and *for* him (Col 1:16). Jesus is the one in whom "all things hold together" (Col 1:17). And it is through this particular man that "God was pleased to reconcile to himself all things, whether on earth or in heaven, by making peace through the blood of his cross" (Col 1:20). Clearly, this hymn declares that "all things" have a place in God's reconciling and redeeming life. All places—from the foothills of southern Alberta to industrial centers like Gary, Indiana—are destined to know the health and salvation of God.

This way of thinking should startle us. Here we are presented with a vision in which nothing escapes God's love and attention. Why? Because God created *everything*. As created by God, the creation is all good and beautiful and of the highest value. But what could it possibly mean to say that a person who lived within the created order—Jesus—is also the one through whom and for whom all creatures came to be? Why should we think that the great diversity of creation holds together in him? And what are the implications of believing that Christ's cross makes possible the peace and reconciliation of all creatures?

Clearly, Jesus is no ordinary person. What Christ accomplishes exceeds the expectations and imaginations of most people. Indeed, part of the good news of the gospel is the fact that we cannot limit God's love. Good news has been proclaimed "to every creature under heaven," which means that the gospel is also intended for every creature and will have its appropriate, divinely desired effect (Col 1:23). What would it look like, practically speaking, to proclaim the gospel to rivers, redwoods, raccoons and roaches? Is our presence on earth good news for all the creatures with which we live?

One of the more striking aspects of this early Christian hymn is its affirmation of material, fleshly life. Here Christ is not reduced to a moral or spiritual teacher who comes down to earth to deliver a few special teachings that will get some of us to heaven. God's life with us, his dwelling with us, does not happen as an immaterial soul-to-soul or mind-to-mind connection. It is body to body, flesh to flesh. What God accomplishes in Christ he accomplishes through blood, the medium of bodily life. God reconciles all the bodies of this world in and by Jesus' "fleshly body through death" (Col 1:22).

What these passages mean, and what practical transformations they entail, we have yet to see. For now, we can determine that this way of speaking sets a baseline for our thinking about the nature of God's reconciliation through Christ: *Christian reconciliation is about bringing all bodies into a peaceful, life-promoting and convivial relationship with each other.* It makes no sense to limit reconciliation to people, let alone individual souls, since we thrive only insofar as we are nurtured, warmed, inspired and protected by the countless bodies of creation that daily touch or circulate through us. The reconciliation of only human souls with each other, however commendable and beautiful, would be an impoverished reconciliation if such souls were consigned to bodies that must eat, drink and breathe their way through a poisoned and degraded creation. Such an incomplete reconciliation would amount to a repudiation of the created earth God loves and daily sustains. It would be a denial of the resurrection power that will bring our bodies into the new heaven and new earth to live with God forever (see Rev 21).

We can spend a lot of time debating whether or not Paul and the early Christians really believed worms, plants and bees to be included in God's salvation of the world. In certain respects, the debate is beside the point. Unless we believe that God cares only about disembodied souls—a position consistently condemned by the church as heretical—then it is all of creation or none of it that God will save. Human life simply makes no sense apart from the life of all creation. We live only because the worms, plants and bees do too. And they live because God loves them.

RESISTING THE SOCRATIC URGE

The allure of Socrates is responsible for the difficulty that many Christians have with the idea that God is reconciling all things in heaven and on earth. Although they may have never read a Socratic dialogue, many people are tempted to follow his teaching about the fate of bodies, which suggests that bodies have no eternal value because they are subject to disease, decay and death, and the source of so much rivalry, disappointment and pain. Think about all the violence the world has known because of envy and lust. The best thing about bodies, in this perspective, is that we can leave them behind when we die. Bodies, in other words, have no place in our future, eternal life.

For Socrates, the main problem with bodies is their materiality. All things material are temporal, changeable and corruptible. Put simply, they are imperfect. That means we cannot count on them to endure or even behave as we want. We have to deal with the fact that the beauty and fitness and health of our bodies, though perhaps enabling a few temporary pleasures, are fleeting phenomena. Though we may be physically attractive to somebody for a time, the time will also come when our bodies will be ravaged by disease and age, thus likely becoming unattractive to others and to us. We will perhaps even come to hate our bodies, seeing in them little but frustration and limit and misery. Having been with medical staff who work with sick and aging patients and who see the disintegration of bodies and minds, I understand why they might say, "It will be a blessed day when this poor soul is freed from her wasting body and confused mind."

This dualistic way of thinking, however, all but inevitably leads to placing our hope in the immortality of the soul. This teaching says that when we die, our souls separate from our bodies. If our souls have been properly prepared—for Socrates, this preparation entailed extensive philosophical training, but for Christians it might take the form of believing the right doctrines or doing the right things—they will then make their flight to a spiritual heaven where they will enjoy the bliss of a life no longer constrained or damaged by imperfect, unruly, disease-ridden and death-bound bodies.

Socratic thinking about bodies has been attractive to Christians for a long time. It is, however, a profoundly anti-Christian way of understanding the world. Why? Because it denies the goodness and beauty of the material world that God so deeply and forever loves. It denies the incarnation of God in the body of Jesus Christ. Thus it falls prey to one of the many gnostic heresies that have either disdained or denied or simply been suspicious of Christ's fleshly life. It denies the Christian hope in the resurrection of the body. It denies John's vision of the new heaven and the new earth in which God's holy city *descends* to earth because "the home of God is among mortals" (Rev 21:3).

From the beginning, God's nurture, love and joy have been revealed and made real in our bodies and in the material bodies of the world. Jesus' body is of supreme, unalterable significance because its materiality—the fact that it could physically touch us and dwell with us—makes possible the healing and the liveliness of every body on earth. Jesus' miracles are not, as modern deists suppose, an "interruption" of the laws governing a body's life; rather, they are the body's *liberation* into wholeness. From a Christian point of view, there can be no Socratic-like hatred of bodies. Rather than seeking an escape from our bodies, we must hope and invest in their healing, reconciliation and redemption.

Notice that a Christian view of the body does not take delight in bodies that are hungry, ill or wasting away. Much of Jesus' ministry was devoted to the feeding, healing and touching of bodies. The Christian Scriptures show us that God's created order is now in a state of pain and suffering. The effects of sin are everywhere visible to us. What the resurrection of Jesus teaches is that this state will not endure, because Christ has overcome sin and death. Christ calls his followers to take up his ministries of nurturing, feeding and healing. In so doing, we bear witness to the God who has never stopped loving the world.

The resurrection of reconciled bodies: this is the gospel's good news. Without it, we and the whole world are lost. Without it, we may grow to despise the creation. The apostle Paul put the matter bluntly: "If there is no resurrection of the dead, then Christ has not been raised; and if Christ has not been raised, then our proclamation has been in vain and your faith has been in vain. We are even found to be misrepresenting God, because we testified of God that he raised Christ" (1 Cor 15:13-15). If Christians believed in the immortality of the soul and the wretchedness of human bodies, the tomb on

Easter morning would not have been empty—because Jesus' body would have remained and only his soul ascended.

Paul knew what was at stake in teaching the resurrection of the body. From his experience at the Athenian Areopagus, he knew that such a radical affirmation of embodiment would provoke the doubt and ridicule of many (see Acts 17:32). To affirm it requires an entirely new way of thinking about God, the inestimable value of the material world and the meaning of life.

FORSAKING THE BODIES OF THE WORLD

The Socratic urge to despise bodies is not the only impediment to understanding God's reconciliation with the whole material world. Another source of our difficulty is that we suffer from *ecological amnesia*. This condition is a fairly recent development in the history of humanity. It is a form of amnesia that, while having a philosophical expression, takes root because of the ways we live in the world. Its most basic cause is the practical separation of people from the land. This separation takes two forms: *physical* (a matter of location) and *existential* (a matter of how we relate to others).

First, many of us are physically separated from the land. More people now live in cities than live on farms. This has never before been the case. Just two generations ago, most people worked on the land, drew their livelihood from it and understood with the certainty of their stomachs that human life is inextricably intertwined with the health of fields, plants, forests and animals. If people were not themselves farmers, they most likely knew or were related to many people who were.

Cities have existed for a very long time, of course, but today's cities are historically unique because of their large size, which tends to insulate inhabitants from agricultural and ecological realities. This means that the people living in them may have no understanding or appreciation for the ecological contexts and responsibilities that make their living possible. Today's forms of urban and suburban life make it likely that people will not appreciate where their food and energy come from and what processes have been used to make them available. They may not understand how easily ecological systems can come to ruin. This is problematic because what people do not see and understand they will less likely value and protect.

Ecologists now tell us that *all* the world's ecosystems are in varying states of crisis. We are eroding our soils and then pounding them with herbicides and fertilizers. We are depleting and poisoning our groundwater. We are felling our forests and contributing to the growth of deserts. Meanwhile, the oceans are warming and becoming more acidic, coral reefs are bleaching and dying, plant and animal species are becoming extinct at a vastly accelerated rate, glaciers and permafrost are melting, and arctic and Antarctic ice sheets are simply disappearing. We did not come to this unprecedented state of affairs by people waking up each morning and plotting to destroy the earth. Instead, we have committed many small acts that we think will improve our standing in this world without realizing their disastrous ecological effects. We have bought into an economic system that depends on and becomes more successful by the destruction of the earth. All around the world there is an alarming inability to see—let alone correct—the effects of our consumer decisions.

For instance, nearly half of the electricity produced in America depends on the burning of coal. The cheapest and most efficient method for getting this coal is called *mountaintop removal*. Rather than sending miners down deep shafts so they can mine coal and send it to the surface, coal companies use explosives to remove layers of a mountain, thus exposing the coal seams to big equipment.

Think of these mountains as if they were very large, irregularly shaped pieces of lasagna. The coal resides in several layers, some in the middle and others near the bottom. You might attempt to drill holes from the top and then siphon the desired layers through these holes. This would take a long time, require considerable expense and is not without many dangers. Rather, why not remove the undesirable levels altogether so as to have more efficient access to the layers you want?

But the mountains are large. You can't neatly remove one layer with the hope of putting it back. To remove each layer requires explosive force—force that forever destroys the vegetation and water tables and the animal and human lives that depend on a healthy ecological system. Although we might have a cheap source of coal as a result of this practice, and thus a cheaper source of electricity—this is usually the consumer's overriding concern—we have forever destroyed an ecosystem to get it. Streams that once provided drinking water and fish are now destroyed and polluted with toxic metals. The forests, the birds and the wildlife are simply gone. Communities are ravaged by unemployment, poisoned water and respiratory illnesses. Heavy trucks hauling the coal degrade the roads. Explosions crack the foundations of homes, and everywhere is the depressing vision of mountain rubble. Promises made on behalf of the land's "reclamation" rarely materialize or are successful.

Destruction of ecosystems did not start with mountaintop removal. What is important to understand, however, is that massive ecological destruction becomes more likely when people are not in a position to see the effects of their decisions. When the location of our increasingly insular and urban living shields us from the harmful effects of our consumer preferences, we are more likely to destroy what we clearly depend on: clean water, healthy forests and vibrant mountain communities. How many of us, living far from the coalfields of Appalachia, know that when we turn on the electric switch we also ignite another explosion in the mountains? Do we understand how our desire for cheap consumer products exhausts our lands and waters and pumps greenhouse gases into our warming atmosphere?

Mountaintop removal is one example of a pattern played over and over again in different settings: in the name of progress or human well-being, we turn against the earth and extract what we want even if it means exhausting, degrading or destroying the sources of life that we and all other creatures need. We fail to appreciate that this logic of exploitation of the land must finally be turned against humanity as well. To degrade the bodies of the earth—its forests, streams, soils, oceans, prairies and mountains—is to degrade the human bodies that depend on them for food, fiber, energy, pleasure and inspiration. This is what the colonial gesture has always been: the enslavement, degradation and destruction of both the land and its people. How can we love a community of people if we are destroying the land on which they live?

While visiting communities in Appalachia, I heard over and over again that mountaintop removal, while clearly an assault on the Appalachian Mountains, is also an assault on its people. Corporate desire for profits and consumer desire for cheap products mean that human and nonhuman bodies must suffer the same fate: abuse. Repeatedly I heard how local sheriffs turned a blind eye to the speeding, overloaded coal trucks that forced cars off the road, causing injury and sometimes death. I heard how Environmental Protection Agency inspectors looked at trickles of orange and black water—the very water that residents needed to bathe, cook and grow food—and declared it fit for consumption. I heard how coal company executives used the threat of job loss to keep residents from speaking out or demanding compensation for destroyed homes and diseased bodies. I heard residents refer to themselves as "throwaway people," as insignificant collateral damage in the march of American economic supremacy. It became clear to me that both the mountains and their people were subject to disappearing acts. One resident lamented that Appalachian people were clearly not as cute as the sea otters that received considerable attention after the Exxon Valdez oil spill. Not being the focus of our attention, the people of Appalachia could not be the focus of our concern either.

Our growing separation from the land and our lack of understanding of the land's integrity result in a growing separation from people. Just as we view land abstractly—as a pile of natural resources—we also come to see people abstractly—as fodder for the growing economy. People cease to matter except if they contribute to a business plan.

If we wanted to demonstrate in a decisive way that the people of Appalachia really matter, we would join with the prophet Isaiah, who spoke of a new, coming creation in which people can again find their material habitats a place of delight: "They shall build houses and inhabit them; they shall plant vineyards and eat their fruit. . . . They shall not labor in vain, or bear children for calamity; for they shall be offspring blessed by the LORD—and their descendants as well" (Is 65:21, 23). In this glorious new creation, the bodies of humanity and the land are not pitted against each other but rather joined in healthy relationships that promote life and joy.

Physical separation from the land is one form of the ecological amnesia that is damaging the world. Its second form is existential: loss of the practical, working relationships that can teach us about our need of other creatures. When we grow food, spin wool or cotton or build and heat a home, we are brought into relationships that can teach us care and respect. We learn how much we depend on fellow creatures for our own lives. We learn that we do not simply or temporarily *have* bodies but that we *live through* bodies that are in constant relationship with other creatures and with God. Although we are clearly more than matter in motion, we are never, not even in our resurrected life, isolated souls.

When we live primarily as consumers, we run the risk of viewing the world as a big store where we can purchase what we choose. As shoppers, we are primarily concerned with whether the store has what we want, when we want it and at an affordable price. Because we are rarely involved in the production of what we need, it is easy to forget that the clothing we buy depends on healthy soils to grow cotton and healthy sheep to provide wool. Or we fail to appreciate that our desire for cheap goods means that farmers and workers will not receive a just wage. Gradually we begin to imagine ourselves as exempt from or beyond ecological realities and agricultural responsibilities. Although we must eat and drink to live— thus daily bearing witness to our attachment to soil, streams, plants and animals—we may start to think that we can have good food and clean water even though mining and industrial agricultural practices steadily poison and deplete the land and its watersheds.

Again, this is a novel development in human history. For most of history, people have been directly involved in the production of their food. Whether as hunters and gatherers or, more likely, as peasants and farmers, people understood that in order to eat, they had to understand and respect the soil, climate, plants and animals. It would have been stupid to foul the water they would eventually drink or abuse the cow that would give them milk, butter, cream, cheese and meat. Although it did not guarantee a fully satisfied or comfortable life, such work refined and reinforced the understanding that survival was deeply implicated in the lives of other creatures. It taught humans that the basis for health and well-being was thoroughly bound up with the health and well-being of the fields, waters and animals that warmed and fed them. In short, this was an understanding of humans as embodied beings in multiple, unfathomably complex relationships with nonhuman bodies.

Although few of us now farm or mill the timber that builds our homes, the most fundamental truth about our lives has not changed: our lives depend on countless seen and unseen, living and dead bodies that touch and nurture our own. Without them we would not be. Although we may no longer be in proximate or practical relationship with the bodies of creation, we still and always will need them. They are the daily source of nurture and joy.

Ecological amnesia is so devastating because it leads us to forsake the material world. It contributes to an impoverished understanding of reconciliation because it trains us to think of ourselves as no longer dependent on clean water, fertile soil, diverse forests and fields and multitudes of insects and animals. As amnesiacs, we live an illusory life. We have forgotten what is not only good but absolutely fundamental: that we are bodies bound to each other through webs of food, water, breath, energy, inspiration, pleasure and delight.

A Created Membership of Bodies

The scriptural account of creation shows us that the Socratic urge and ecological amnesia are damaging. It can also lead us into the fullness of our embodied life together. If we hope to live into a Christian vision of reconciliation, we need to recover an understanding of ourselves as creatures in relationship with other creatures, all of us dependent on God.

To grasp the deep and practical significance of this teaching, we must first recognize that the Bible does not describe the world as nature. Though *nature* is a complex term having many different meanings, for many people (Christians included) the environment is an amoral realm of material stuff that functions according to natural laws. These laws are impersonal, operating on matter that has value insofar as we assign it. According to this view, nature provides us with the resources we need to live well; it is the backdrop that facilitates the ambitions and dramas we live.

A great number of people believe that God matters because God is the one who created nature. God's creative act, though clearly very important, is assumed to be past tense. Within this perspective, the world and all its elements, inhabitants and processes have moved according to laws that God designed long ago. Although God may be evident in the complexity and order of the world's design, God's presence is no longer necessary. Nature runs by itself. If God appears at all, it is in the form of a miracle, understood as God's *interruption* of the laws and processes that otherwise function quite well on their own.

Is it appropriate, theologically speaking, to think about the world this way? Although an understanding of the world as nature may make room for a god as its origin, it has little room for an understanding of nature as having its end or goal in God. This is because modern science eliminated *teleology*, the idea that the natural world is moving toward any identifiable and valuable end. The physical, chemical, biological and evolutionary laws that have produced the wonderful diversity on this earth do not tell us anything about how the world *should* be or what its ultimate destiny is. That all the elements of the world should one day be reconciled with each other and with God—even Psalm 104's foundational idea that God is constantly present to creatures as their animating breath— exceeds what the natural sciences allow us to say.

The story of creation in Genesis 1 is well known—probably too well known. We often take it for granted, thus missing essential dimensions of its unfolding. As the story goes, each day is marked by God creating something new: light (day one), a water-separating dome (day two), dry, vegetation-producing earth and gathered waters (day three), the sun and moon (day four), self-multiplying creatures of the sea and birds of the air (day five), wild and domestic land animals and humankind, made in the image of God and called to have dominion over all the creatures that move (day six). For many people, this is where the story stops. After all, Genesis 2:1 suggests that after the six days "the heavens and the earth were finished, and all their multitude."

This rendition of the story does not dwell enough on day

seven: the day of Sabbath, which marks the fulfillment of the creation story. This is the day blessed and hallowed by God. It is the day on which God rests.

Why does God rest? Is it because God is tired? We need to think carefully about this, because God's resting in creation is the key to creation's deep and inner meaning. In other words, unless we understand why God rests and what God's resting looks like, we won't know what creation is about and what it is ultimately *for*.

As long as we characterize rest as inactivity or the cessation of work, we will misunderstand it. Rest is not about escaping from the work world. Nor is it about "checking out" from our many cares. Why? Because God never departs from us or desires an escape from this world. God is constantly present to every creature, animating it from within. As the psalmist put it, God is the breath within our breath, giving us life and forever renewing the face of the ground. The day God turns his face away from us is also the day on which we die and return to the dust of the ground (see Ps 104:29-30).

So much of our thinking about rest is off the mark because we lack the love that God has for everything. We desire to check out because we are bored or comfortably numb. Or we find the work we do so degrading or meaningless to others and to ourselves that we can't wait to be done with it.

None of this fatigue or boredom or degradation pertains to God. When God looks out on creation on the first Sabbath sunrise, he sees a good and beautiful and fruitful world. Repeatedly in Genesis 1, we find God seeing how good the creation is. There is a palpable excitement building as God completes each day, because with each day yet another wonderful creation is completed. When God considers any creature, what God sees is a physical manifestation of his own love.

Understood in this Sabbath light, God's rest is not a departure from this world but the fullest and most intimate immersion in it. When God practices *Shabbat,* God takes complete delight in what is made. Delight marks the moment when we find whatever is in our presence so lovely and so good that there is no other place we want to be. All we want to do is soak it up, be fully present to it and cherish the goodness of the world God has made. Something so good cannot be enjoyed from a distance or in the abstract. It requires the deep knowledge that comes from union, from the tasting of it. The Latin word for "knowledge," *sapere,* also means "to taste." It even suggests erotic intimacy, since the Hebrew word for "knowledge" also connotes sexual union. Delight is inspired by the love that receives and enjoys another in his or her or its divinely bestowed loveliness.

The opposite of rest is not work but restlessness. We are restless in both our work and our entertainment because we find them unsatisfying and not contributing to the fullness of life. We are restless in our consumption, always wanting more and better, because we think what we currently have is not good enough. Ours is a restless economy because it can find no contentment in its frenzied and destructive engagement with anything. This restlessness leads directly to the neglect of the places we are in and the people we are with.

A scriptural account of creation, one that finds its completion in God's own Sabbath delight, is so important for us to understand because it shows how readily we mis*take* the creatures of the world. We need this teaching more than ever so we can come to know what creatures really *are*. No creature, no body whatsoever, should be neglected, despised or abused. Each body is God's love made visible, touchable, smellable, hearable and delectable. God desires the reconciliation of all bodies in heaven and on earth, because it is in such reconciliation that God's never-ending love is fully witnessed. Nothing in God's creation is to be despised or forgotten. All that is exists for the glory of God. God the Creator is glorified in the liveliness and loveliness of the created world.

That we are embodied creatures dependent on the nurture, warmth and inspiration of each other is not a sign of weakness or insufficiency. The bodily relationships we live through—as when we are fed by others, nurtured by others, healed by others, inspired by others or comforted by others—are instead God's way of showing us his physical, material love. God invites us through Christ to participate in this reconciling love, and in so doing bring peace to all things in heaven and on earth.

God has given to us a ministry of reconciliation. It is a ministry founded on Christ's reconciling of the whole world to himself (see 2 Cor 5:18-19). Far from being limited to individual, disembodied souls, his is a reconciliation of all the material bodies of creation. It is a ministry that begins with, and continually returns to, reconciliation with the land.

2

Learning to See

FRED BAHNSON

*I*t is now Eastertide. In the small church where I worship, a man in the choir sings a solo refrain during the Great Thanksgiving. The man is blind. I do not know his name, but each week I listen for the rich sound of his voice. The blind man's solo refrain comes just before the priest lifts up the elements, and this is what he sings: *the disciples knew the Lord Jesus in the breaking of the bread.*

I've been thinking about that line, which alludes to the Emmaus story in Luke's Gospel, in which two disciples walked with Jesus along the road, "but their eyes were kept from recognizing him" (Lk 24:16). It was only when they sat at the table with Jesus that the disciples saw him. *The disciples knew the Lord Jesus in the breaking of the bread.*

After the consecration of the elements, I watch the blind

man come to the altar to receive Christ's body and blood. The man's seeing-eye dog steps beside his master at the communion rail, and as he shakes his leash, I think about blindness. What keeps us from perceiving the world as it should be? What will open our eyes so that we see things as Jesus desires them to be seen? As I watch the blind man with the lovely voice return to his seat in the choir, I'm reminded that his physical blindness is not how Jesus desires things should be. That's why Jesus healed people like him.

But while the man in the choir may lack physical sight, most of us suffer from blindness of a different sort. It's a blindness Norman described as ecological amnesia: an inability to see the rest of the created order that Jesus has already reconciled to himself and an inability to see the harm we're causing it.

As I yearn to rid myself of my own blindness, I've been turning to poets. The intensity of vision I find in good poetry helps me to refine my own. At its best, poetry is not flowery language or wordplay. It is a way of seeing—which is to say, a way of knowing. Lately I've been rereading the poem "YHWH's Image" by one of my favorite writers, the Orthodox poet Scott Cairns. It's a midrashic sort of poem, a riff on Genesis 1:26: "Then God said, 'Let us make humankind in our image, according to our likeness.'" Before reading this poem, I had subconsciously imported the creation story from Genesis 2 back into Genesis 1: God molds clay into the shape of a human, breathes into it and creates a person. But Genesis 1 doesn't describe *how* God made the first humans, male and female; it simply says that God created them in his image.

In Cairns's poem, we see YHWH resting, enjoying what he had created thus far. "Then YHWH lay back, running His hands over the damp grasses, and in deep concentration reached into the soil, lifting great handsful of trembling clay to His lips, which parted to avail another breath." Note that the clay is still unformed. And here we arrive at the heart of the poem: "With this clay He began to coat His shins, cover His thighs, His chest. He continued this layering, and, when He had been wholly interred, He parted the clay at His side, and retreated from it, leaving the image of Himself to wander in what remained of that early morning mist."

What a striking image. YHWH covering himself with breath-filled clay, then retreating from his shell to reveal a new creature. God's own image—us.

This poem changed the way I think about that mysterious phrase "image of God." It's a poetic rendering of Augustine's phrase *terra animata*—"animated earth." How might we look out on a world groaning in labor pains if we remind ourselves that the visage we present to that world is God's own image, moving among the trees and fields, the highways and cities of our time?

This poem points to the kind of imagination we will need if we're to mitigate the damage we've inflicted on the soil and thus on ourselves. It reminds us that we come from YHWH and we come from soil. *Adam* from *adamah*, human from humus. Our relationship with the humus from which we were formed is deeply broken. The earth's sixth great species extinction event is already underway, with humans as the primary cause. We remove entire mountains to light and heat our homes, leading to the destruction of rural communities and ecosystems. The number of hungry people in the world—at the time of this writing, around one billion—is now equaled by the number of obese people. This means that one in three of God's image-bearers are suffering because of either how little they eat or how much they eat. In addition, we are conducting a grand experiment unprecedented in human history: warming the atmosphere beyond its capacity to correct itself. We are already seeing the results of this in freak tornadoes in the Midwest, record drought in Russia, ice-free summers in the Arctic and record temperatures around the globe.

I worry that the church still thinks of these disparate problems as isolated incidents rather than manifestations of the same underlying malady. At some fundamental level, the church views the current ecological crisis as yet another Christian special-interest area. It's just one more side dish on an already groaning potluck table, no more in need of sampling than the other offerings at the Christian smorgasbord: your tastes might lead you to ecological issues, but I'm more interested in Reformation history, say, or Wesleyan studies or liturgical dance.

Meanwhile the Gulf of Mexico is a cesspool of oil and dispersants from the Deepwater Horizon oil spill, the Fukushima Daiichi nuclear meltdown continues to contaminate Japan, and tornadoes exacerbated by climate change are razing entire towns. And on it goes.

As a growing list of scientific reports now tells us, these

events are not random. They are part of the same insidious pattern, the natural outworking of our own hubris. Consider this summary of the Millennium Ecosystem Assessment: "Over the past 50 years, humans have changed ecosystems more rapidly and extensively than in any comparable period of time in human history, largely to meet rapidly growing demands for food, fresh water, timber, fiber, and fuel. This has resulted in a substantial and largely irreversible loss in the diversity of life on Earth."

Here is the much-heralded and little-heeded 2008 report from the International Assessment of Agricultural Knowledge, Science, and Technology for Development (IAASTD). This landmark four-year study, undertaken by the World Bank, the United Nations' Food and Agriculture Organization and multiple stakeholders in the private and nonprofit sectors, called for a complete overhaul of the world's food and farming systems. It declared unequivocally that industrial farming methods are detrimental to the earth's ecosystems and are unable to feed a growing world population, and that we must therefore turn to organic, ecologically sound farming practices as soon as possible.

Because our industrial farming practices have created an overabundance of cheap calories, many of us are dying because of the way we eat. The Centers for Disease Control estimates that, of the children born after 2000, one in three will develop type 2 diabetes.

The National Oceanic and Atmospheric Association tells us the following: "2010 tied with 2005 as the warmest year of the global surface temperature record, beginning in 1880. This was the 34th consecutive year with global temperatures above the 20th century average."

In his book *Eaarth: Making a Life on a Tough New Planet,* Bill McKibben, a Methodist Sunday school teacher from Vermont who is also the world's foremost environmentalist, puts it bluntly: "We're running Genesis backward, de-creating."

A picture emerges from these different reports: the image of a world gone awry. We are YHWH's image-bearers in creation, carrying the standard of YHWH on our visage and given the task of stewarding what YHWH called "good." Yet we are now in the process of decreating much of that goodness. We have wandered far from that early morning mist, far east of Eden.

In the face of all this depressing decreating, what does it mean for the church to proclaim the cosmic scope of Christ's saving work? How can we profess as Lord the one in whom "all things hold together" (Col 1:17) while the work of our hands begets a world in which "things fall apart"? As Norman wrote earlier, we suffer from an impoverished imagination. At some fundamental level, we fail to see the world as God would have us see it.

THE LANGUAGE OF SOIL: A VOCATIONAL JOURNEY

Norman and I both grew up in the West. Norman was raised on the great plains of Alberta, whose amber waves of grain look west toward the glorious Canadian Rockies. Further south down the Rocky Mountain chain, where the peaks are a tad smaller though no less glorious than the ones within view of Norman's boyhood home, sit the mountains of Big Sky Country. Southwestern Montana is as beautiful a place as I've ever known. Although that place has become overrun with fly fishermen, billionaire media tycoons and rubber-tomahawk-seeking tourists in their RVs, the Montana of my boyhood was little known and largely untrammeled. It was a kind of paradise. If we have wandered far east of Eden, I didn't know it then. Our experience of a place matters in how we are formed. (This is not to say that growing up in Montana puts you closer to God than someone who grew up in, say, Alberta. But it helps.)

As a young man I roamed all over Montana's mountains: bow hunting for elk in the Crazies, telemark skiing in the Bridgers, rock climbing in the Spanish Peaks and ice climbing in the Hyalites. These were not elite pursuits; for years I subsisted on minimum-wage jobs in order to spend more time outside, as did many other "soul sport" athletes who lived in Bozeman. In my twenties I began to focus exclusively on alpine climbing. I made trips up and down the hemisphere, going as far north as the Icefields Parkway in Norman's country and as far south as the Cordillera Real range in the Bolivian Andes. The mountains were my church, a climbing rope my rosary, and I approached my spiritual discipline with all the intensity of a monastic oblate fulfilling his holy vows. I tested myself against mountains, learned much from them and lost a dear friend to them. But climbing as a spiritual vehicle, much less as an end in itself, ultimately failed to satisfy. Mountains,

I learned, aren't worth dying for.

At some point, the pastor at a Lutheran church I'd begun attending noted my interest in theology and encouraged me to go to divinity school. Duke would be a good place to seek my vocation, he said. He was hoping I'd end up behind a pulpit, I think. But then I started reading Wendell Berry and began to wonder if God wasn't calling me to the plow (or rather, to the digging spade, since plows destroy soil structure).

After graduating from divinity school in 2000, I lived as a peace worker with a group of Mayan coffee farmers in Chiapas, Mexico. It was there that I glimpsed a life lived close to the land. It was a life of poverty, to be certain, and I didn't romanticize it. But it was a life of beauty and integrity nonetheless, a life made lovely by the close connection my new Mayan friends had with the soil. A life I wanted as my own. When I returned from Chiapas in 2001, I volunteered on a permaculture farm in Chatham County, North Carolina, where I learned the skills necessary to grow my own food. During that year I met my future wife. We bought a small acreage and began to refine our skills of horticulture and husbandry. We raised a few dairy goats, a pair of hogs we named Chorizo and Chuletta ("Sausage" and "Pork Chop"), several hundred broilers and a few slaughter lambs. We learned to garden year-round—not only during the summer months of bounty, during which we would can tomatoes and freeze pole beans, but also during the winter months, which farmer-writer Eliot Coleman calls "the backside of the calendar."

We learned much during these experiments in cottage

farming. I used to think that if you wanted to be a real farmer, you had to like animals. Maybe that's true. But animals, I learned, mostly frustrated me. I liked plants. Plants don't die after getting their head stuck in a fence, like one of our sheep did. Plants don't attack you, like our big tom turkey did until we gave him to an unsuspecting neighbor. Elizabeth was drawn to the animals, but plants proved to be my calling, and during those early years of learning the agrarian arts, I took as much pleasure in my failures at gardening as I did my successes. Sometimes I would even forget to harvest a crop, so rapt was I by the process of growing it. To this day Elizabeth is still the one who harvests food from our garden. Having successfully brought a crop to maturity, I've by then lost interest and have moved on to planting a cover crop or turning a compost pile.

In 2005 my theological training, writing and love of growing food came together when I was invited to help a rural Methodist church in Cedar Grove, North Carolina, start a community garden. We called it Anathoth Community Garden, after the little field God told Jeremiah to purchase during the Babylonian siege of Jerusalem. Our mission also came from Jeremiah, to "plant gardens and eat what they produce. . . . seek the peace of the city where I have sent you into exile, and pray to the LORD on its behalf, for in its peace you will find your peace" (Jer 29:5, 7). During the four years I directed this church-supported agriculture ministry, I became even more convinced that feeding people is a holy calling, as Jesus' last words to Peter make clear (see Jn 21:15-17). In 2009 my wife and I moved with our young children to be closer to extended family. We are now in the early stages of creating a half-acre edible forest garden in the mountains of western North Carolina, which we hope will not only feed our family but also be a teaching center. My work now is to write about what I've learned on the land. Since those early days at Anathoth, I have come to see that caring for soil and caring for words—both ways of feeding people—are my twin vocations. It is my prayer that the church will encourage such vocations among more of its members, for we will need many more people who are agriculturally literate in the years ahead.

My vocational journey of learning to see has only just begun. My journey's arc is downward, a geographical descent that began in the high peaks of Montana and dropped to the mountains of Mexico, finally settling in the hills and valleys of western North Carolina. Rather than looking to the airy heights for transcendence, I find myself looking for God's kingdom come down where the earthworms are slowly building soil. I want to crouch with Jesus there in the dust, where he still scribbles "a word not yet perceived." I am still blind, seeing only through a glass darkly. I want to be granted the gift of sight.

INTIMACY WITH THE LAND

It's been more than ten years since I gave up climbing, renouncing my membership in what one writer has called the "First Church of the Higher Elevations." But while I came to see the inadequacy of seeking God apart from the body of Christ, I carry with me from my climbing years this unshakable conviction: God created us not only for intimacy with God and with others but for intimacy with the land. There is no golden era to harken back to, no time of harmony we can pine for, because we've been abusing the land ever since leaving Eden. Agrarians like Wes Jackson say that agriculture is a ten-thousand-year-old bad habit, our original sin, because it allowed us to start drawing down "the capital stock of the planet."

Yet at least the results of our ecological sin—that eroded gully above the village, this overirrigated field next to the river—were visible. We may not have recognized it as sin, but we would still have to face the results. Now, however, most of us live in built environments so that we don't even see what we're doing. Food simply appears on the shelves, and we don't see the deep rills of erosion in the Palouse region of Washington from excessive tillage or the plume of algae creating a dead zone in the Gulf of Mexico from fertilizer runoff. Lights come on at the flip of a switch, but we don't see the groundwater poisoned from hydrofracking or the mountaintop blown apart to extract the coal. We may be shocked over isolated instances like the Deepwater Horizon or Fukushima Daiichi accidents, but mostly the ecological costs of our way of life remain a distant background noise, something for ecologists and people who love polar bears to worry about.

Let's bracket, for a moment, the slow unraveling of the thread of life that's taking place right outside our window and look at what our ecological amnesia does to *us*. We have to wonder what we're missing when we've so arranged our world that we don't need to know where our food or the energy to heat our homes or our clothing comes from. We don't need to know how the person who picked our tomatoes was treated. I can become an expert at programming software or writing a codicil to a will, and I will be paid handsomely for it, far more than the person who feeds me. I will never have to learn the first thing about where my food comes from. I will not need to learn the best time to start fall broccoli seeds (early July here in zone 7) or what is the best carbon-to-nitrogen ratio for a thermophilic compost pile (thirty to one). I can ignore everything about my food, my shelter and the ambient temperature of my home except how much coin of the realm I must shell out to get it.

What's missing? Not much, you might say. Most people are pretty happy not to have to worry about these things. After all, a worry-free lifestyle is one of the cornerstones of modern life that needs no defense. The story we moderns tell ourselves goes something like this: once upon a time our ancestors lived lives of drudgery. They toiled on the land for their food. They had little time for leisure. They pretty much just suffered a lot. Then came industrialization and modern agriculture, which freed most of us from the burdens of manual labor and food production. In advanced industrial societies like ours, most of us are specialists in particular areas of expertise: farmer, lawyer, carpenter, pastor, homemaker, computer programmer and so on. Our society of specialists takes care of our basic needs, and therefore we don't need to know how to look after ourselves, feed ourselves and clothe ourselves; we can pay somebody to do that. We can thankfully get on with other "higher" pursuits.

But perhaps we've been telling each other the wrong story. What is missing is our intimacy with God, which is closely linked to our intimacy with the land.

Land was a given for the biblical writers. The Bible is not a *green* book insofar as *green* names some kind of environmental action plan or conscientious shopping guide. Land was a given for the biblical writers, because they knew that land was an implicit part of their relationship with God. The possibility for shalom on the land, Israel knew, was dependent on their obedience to God. "If you will only heed his every commandment that I am commanding you today—loving the LORD your God, and serving him with all your heart and with all your soul—then he will give the rain for your land in its season, the early rain and the later rain, and you will gather in your grain, your wine, and your oil; and he will give grass in your fields for your livestock, and you will eat your fill" (Deut 11:13-15).

The land is implicit in Jesus' ministry as well. Just as YHWH scooped up the land to form the first Adam, YHWH's Son scooped up the land to perform the mighty works recorded in the Gospels. Jesus' healing flowed from the land into people through the media of soil, water, saliva, bread and fish. His ministry took place not in the airless confines of the temple but in the open hill country of Galilee: mountaintops, olive gardens, lakes, rivers, wilderness. It is only we moderns who think of these physical places as quaint backdrops, interchangeable stage settings on which the real action takes place—the preaching and praying, the baptizing and converting, the healing and resurrecting. Yet the mystery of the incarnation means that these places are inseparable from the story itself. They are also a part of the incarnation of Christ. Indeed, the atoms and molecules of the Galilean hill country went into Jesus' body and came out of it as well. Likewise, the soils and watersheds and air are a part of our own salvation narrative.

The theology I read at Duke challenged me to think about my relationship with God as inextricably a part of the larger body of Christ. But as much as I learned from them, something important was missing when I read Karl Barth, Søren Kierkegaard or John Howard Yoder. To find that something, I turned to poets and novelists with land sensibility, writers like Wendell Berry, Annie Dillard and Barry Lopez.

In his book *Home Ground: Language for an American Landscape,* Lopez writes: "[M]any American poets and novelists have recognized that something emotive abides in the land, and that it can be recognized and evoked even if it cannot be thoroughly plumbed. It is inaccessible to the analytic researcher, invisible to the ironist. To hear the unembodied call of a place, that numinous voice, one has to wait for it to speak through the harmony of its features—the soughing of the wind across it, its upward reach against a clear night sky, its fragrance after a rain."

Lopez is a "secular" writer whose land sensibility is, I think, more akin to the biblical writers than that of most modern

Christians. What Lopez would call "something emotive" abiding in the land the Deuteronomist would call *Shekhinah* and Paul would call the *Paraclete*. It is the indwelling and felt presence of the Lord mediated through the physical world. I think of Job, listening to the Lord speak out of the whirlwind; of Elijah, his face wrapped in a mantle, waiting for God to pass by his cave entrance on Mount Horeb; of John the Revelator, receiving his vision on the remote island of Patmos. Some would write off these events as myth, something the biblical writers invented to make a point. If we take a more literal view of Scripture, we assume that such events happened but that they occurred "back then." Nowadays God might strangely warm our hearts during a particularly rousing stanza of "The Old Rugged Cross," but unless we're Pentecostals, that's about as much *Shekhinah* as we can expect.

What if climate change, species depletion and the long litany of ecological woes were, at root, an inability to acknowledge or feel God's presence in the land? If there were coal under Mount Horeb, Sinai or another place we associate with God's presence, would we remove that mountain to get at it? And is God any less present in the mountains we remove in West Virginia, or the waters we poison in the Gulf of Mexico or the topsoil we squander through industrial farming practices?

Reconciliation with the land means learning to see the land as part of God's redemptive plan and acknowledge God's ongoing presence there. That will require putting ourselves in proximity to the land and staying there long enough to be changed.

Again, Lopez: "One must wait for the moment when the

thing—the hill, the tarn, the lunette, the kiss tank, the caliche flat, the bajada—ceases to be a thing and becomes something that knows we are there." To believe that Jesus Christ has redeemed the cosmos is to say that he has redeemed the land on which he lived and the land on which you and I live. Every hill and tarn, every caliche flat and bajada, every mountaintop we might remove and every seam of coal inside it: these have *already been reconciled* (see Col 1:20). Our failure to see this constitutes the "not yet" in which sin retains its stranglehold. But with God's help, we can begin to see. Even a glimpse could be enough to fuel a lifetime's work of restoration.

We must be clear, though: we aren't trying to reclaim a lost paradise; rather, we should welcome the New Jerusalem. We're gardening toward the *parousia*. The gospel points us toward a new garden kingdom we're to seek, a heavenly kingdom that breaks into our damaged Eden. Its marks are restored relationships between people, yes. But for it to really be the kingdom of God, it must also demonstrate restored relationships with the actual land on which actual people live. Otherwise it remains a kingdom of gnostics, whose heads float five feet above the ground and who never quite feel the earth beneath their feet. We're heading not only toward a new heaven but a new earth as well (see Rev 21). Our work, then, must anticipate and be the firstfruits of this new earth. The way we care for the soil should take on an eschatological awareness if we're to be reconciled with it. Reconciliation with the land will require skills, habits and patterns of living that align our lives more fully with that of Christ. And that requires training in the virtue of humility.

THE GREAT TRANSITION

In her essay "Wilderness," Marilynne Robinson writes, "I think we are desperately in need of a new, chastened, self-distrusting vision of the world, an austere vision that can postpone the outdoor pleasures of cherishing exotica, and the first-world pleasures of assuming we exist to teach reasonableness to the less fortunate, and the debilitating pleasures of imagining that our own impulses are reliably good." What Robinson is calling for in biblical terms is humility: a fundamental distrust of our own power and motives and a recognition that we are completely reliant on God.

This reminds me of something my friend Ragan Sutterfield said recently. Ragan lives in Little Rock, Arkansas. Like me, Ragan is a writer, subsistence gardener and purveyor of doomsday literature (in roughly that order). For a while Ragan ran his own farm, selling pasture-raised poultry, pork, lamb and beef. He then helped to found Felder Farm, an urban educational farm for youth. Lately we've been exchanging letters, the old-fashioned, handwritten sort, the kind that you must stop what you're doing for an hour and put some thought into in order to write. In these letters, we update each other on all the great gardening we're doing and all the great writing we plan to do but are not doing. Mostly we try to understand what I called above our underlying malady. I want to quote at length from one of his letters, because I think Ragan is trying to articulate the kind of chastened, self-distrusting vision we need for the times ahead:

> I've been thinking a good deal lately about reality, because I've been thinking about both the abstraction of our lives and humility. Bernard of Clairvaux says that humility is "living in the truth," and I keep thinking about that and comparing it to the systems and institutions that surround us and seem to insulate us from the truth. For those who live in cities and deal almost entirely in a money economy in which work produces an abstract value that is then used to purchase goods and services; for those people it is hard to imagine how something like soil biology or nutrient cycles could be made meaningful—they are almost alien. What I think is perhaps the most important witness for Christians in this sort of abstract world is to be carnal—to be embodied and concrete, to do work that leaves calluses and sore muscles, or at least ink stains.

At a practical level, our ecological amnesia is a luxury we can no longer afford. The lifestyle we have adopted for the past fifty years or so is one we can't sustain. Given the challenges of oil depletion, climate disruption, resource scarcity and failing ecosystems, our amnesiac approach to life is not going to serve us very well in the years ahead.

In October 2009, I spent a few days with Wes Jackson, a MacArthur Fellow, founder of The Land Institute and winner of the Right Livelihood Award. Jackson has spent the past thirty years thinking about land, energy, food and climate—in short, thinking about the forces that sustain our life on earth. Based on our current rates of extraction, Jackson believes the only way forward is to "down-power," to greatly curtail our use of fossil energy. "We're in a great transition, the most important in human history," he told me. "Anyone who died before 1930 never lived through a doubling of the human population. Anyone born after 2050 likely won't either. We are in a 120-year period of transition that will require an emerging consciousness if we're going to make it through." Jackson wryly noted that we're on the tail end of that 120-year period.

Reconciling with the land in our age will mean looking to the land as a model for how we derive our energy and how we grow our food. Perhaps what we need is for computer programmers, lawyers, economists and, yes, even theologians to direct their creativity toward things like permaculture, biointensive gardening and solar energy—systems that build ecological resilience. In a world of diminishing fossil fuels, climate disruption and eroding topsoil, a lot more us are going to need to put our minds and digging spades to work learning how to feed ourselves and our neighbor. "Nothing can take the place of absolute contact, of seeing and feeding at God's table for oneself," wrote John Muir. "The Lord himself must anoint eyes to see, my pen cannot. One can only see by loving."

Another Eastertide Sunday is approaching, and I am eager to hear the blind man in the choir take up his refrain, one we ourselves will take up in the remaining chapters: *the disciples knew the Lord Jesus in the breaking of the bread.* Just as my fellow church member will bring his blindness to the altar, I will bring mine and you can bring yours. There at the Lord's table, we can pray together the prayer of Bartimaeus in Mark 10:51: "My teacher, let me see."

3

Reconciliation Through Christ

NORMAN WIRZBA

*C*edar Grove is a one-stoplight community in the northern part of Orange County, North Carolina. It has a post office, a church and a bait-and-tackle shop down the road. Nestled in the middle of gently rolling terrain, woodlots and beautiful farmland, it does not draw much attention to itself. Farmers have worked this land for generations, sending their children to school and to church. Residents are currently working to revive an abandoned general store by turning it into an arts and crafts center that will showcase area talent and sell locally produced goods. Viewed from the outside, Cedar Grove is peaceful, even a bit idyllic.

Life changed for this community on a summer afternoon in 2004 when Bill King, the owner of a convenience store, was shot in the back of the head. Bill had recently taken over the store that for years had been a home for crack dealers and drug addicts. He had made the place safe for children to come and eat ice cream, buy candy and drink sodas. He let neighbors buy food on credit when they didn't have the money to pay. His generosity and work ethic were known and admired throughout the community.

Bill's murder was a great shock. Residents wondered if it was racially motivated, since Bill, a white man, was married to Emma, a black woman. The police found a body and an empty cash register, but they were never able to identify a suspect. As far as the people of Cedar Grove knew, the killer was still roaming about the region.

How does a community like Cedar Grove recover from a murder like this? What would reconciliation or peace look like, and what would it require? Exactly who or what needs to be reconciled?

When we probe any community deeply, we can find multiple sources of trouble that, under particular circumstances, might lead to a violent outcome. Most of our lands and communities bear the scars of racial and ethnic oppression, class antagonism, nomadic careerism, neighborhood neglect and greedy ambition. Much of what we claim as personal and communal success depends on the exploitation of soil and water, forests and oceans, chickens and cows—what we have learned to call the earth's "natural resources." In abusing these gifts and sources of life, however, we also end up abusing the human bodies and communities that depend on them. We cannot poison the ground that grows our food without also poisoning its eaters.

Our culture trains us to think that exploitation is "normal," the way things are. That is why we are not surprised or grieved when we learn that the living conditions of many migrant agricultural workers are akin to our slaveholding past, or that poor people living in rural communities—often referred to as "white trash" or "hicks"—lack basic necessities like running water and adequate food. Our land is a place where opulent wealth exists in close proximity to abject poverty. Our country reduces almost everything—from farm fields to lambs to workers—to an economic equation or political advantage. It is a breeding ground for fear, suspicion, abuse and sometimes murder.

But not always. In Cedar Grove, Valee Taylor, a black man, approached Grace Hackney, a white woman, seeking to find a way to address this murder. Valee was hoping to raise money for a reward to capture the killer. But after further conversation, they both decided that was not the right response. As pastor of Cedar Grove United Methodist church, Grace approached Emma, Bill's wife, asking what the church could do for her. Emma did not have enough money to pay for a funeral, so they decided to hold a vigil instead at the parking lot of the store on the two-week anniversary of the murder.

Over one hundred people came: blacks and whites and Latinos, poor and rich, churchgoers and those who had never been in a church. The community gathered to listen to preachers and to remember Bill. People prayed. People cried. People who had never shaken each other's hands or even said hello to each other hugged. For Valee and Grace it was a special moment, a divinely inspired moment, that showed them that the segregation of the past was not normal or inevitable.

Scenobia Taylor, Valee's seventy-six-year-old mother, was at the vigil. A fifth-generation African American descendant of sharecroppers and the daughter of one of Orange County's largest landowners, Scenobia had experienced a lot of racial hatred during her life. Crosses had been burned on her front yard and gun shots fired at her and other children during school integration efforts. But at the vigil, Scenobia saw a new, racially reconciled community being born. Not long after the vigil, she received a vision from God that she should give five acres of land to help feed the hungry. As she put it: "My father, he gave land for a school. My grandfather, he gave land for the church, and for people to be buried. And here, Papa, at one time he had a thousand acres. And then here we all have all this land here. And then what do we do with it? We not doin' nothin'. I wanted to do something like you know my grandfather and my father did, you know. And I just pray, and I were praying and I said Lord, please show me, give me a sign or somethin'."

Land was at the heart of her vision for reconciliation.

Meanwhile, Grace had been dreaming with her church about how they could be involved in the feeding of Cedar Grove's rural poor. Again, land was a central issue. It did not seem right that there should be hungry people in an agricultural community that had good land and the skill to grow good food. Scenobia's vision and Grace's dream, along with the conversations of several community members, came together in the founding of Anathoth Community Garden, a five-acre garden and orchard located just down the road from Bill's store.

The naming of Anathoth Community Garden came from the prophet Jeremiah. Jeremiah was living in a time when his own people had been invaded and sent off to live in Babylonian exile. In the midst of this devastation, fear and violence, God instructed Jeremiah to buy a field at Anathoth as a sign of hope that God would turn devastation into peaceful living. God said a remarkable thing: "Build houses and live in them; plant gardens and eat what they produce. . . . Seek the welfare [*shalom*] of the city where I have sent you into exile, and pray to the LORD on its behalf, for in its welfare you will find your welfare" (Jer 29:5, 7).

Members of the Cedar Grove community took this seriously. With the help of some grants, and under the leadership of Fred, they together turned Scenobia's five acres into a fruitful garden producing thousands of pounds of strawberries, asparagus, tomatoes, greens, blueberries, corn, potatoes and squash. This food is grown with the helping hands of rich and poor, white and black. It is food that is generously shared with shut-ins who have no access to healthy, organically grown produce. It is eaten together at picnic and kitchen tables. Gradually, through hard work and ample conversations, the distance between people is being bridged. Though hardly perfect—tensions and divisions within the community can still be found, and funding and physical energy to keep the garden going are a perennial challenge—Anathoth is a beacon of what is possible when community members are inspired by God's reconciling ways. On special days, it offers a taste of heaven.

What I mean by a "taste of heaven" happened four years ago on a warm fall night. Over one hundred people of every color and class gathered for a potluck celebration at the garden. Much of the food came fresh from the garden, and so included some of the best salsa and greens I have ever tasted. A late afternoon shower had passed through earlier, leaving a dark sky and a double rainbow in its wake. Children ran around laughing and blowing bubbles. Adults listened and danced to the sounds of a live bluegrass band. It was an evening none of us wanted to end. I asked Fred if he had envisioned a night like this as he prepared the ground and put in the first crop of seeds. "Not in my wildest dreams!" he said.

The stories of Jeremiah's Anathoth field and Cedar Grove's Anathoth Community Garden help us see that peace and reconciliation, the mutual flourishing and convivial communality that Jewish people call *shalom*, is a deep and all-embracing reality. Rather than being simply the absence of violence, reconciliation takes us to a physical place—a plot of land—that puts down roots, produces food, provides stability and hospitality, fosters healthy relationships and inspires joy. Shalom presupposes people living securely in the land, which means that land and people *together* are being respected and nurtured. God's reconciling vision results in the safe settlement of people who have been planted by God in the soil and who honor God in all that they do (see Jer 32:37-41).

RECONCILIATION *THROUGH* CHRIST

That everyone will desire or choose a path to reconciliation should not be assumed. People can decide that life is hard, antagonisms are inevitable and that abuse is the natural accompaniment of a successful pursuit. The American dream, after all, is constantly reminding us of the need to "get ahead." For some to be ahead, others must fall behind and be forgotten.

Community members of Cedar Grove certainly did not need to choose a path of reconciliation. They could have turned the murder case over to law officials and invested in personal security systems. When told that little could be done to apprehend the murder suspect, they could have resigned themselves to a justice system that works harder and better for those who have influence and money. They could have given into the despair of self-pity and helplessness.

But they didn't. Members of this community, many of whom had been formed by the Christian story, understood deep down that life is supposed to be more than what our culture tells us is normal. Choosing between reconciled and suspicious forms of life requires that we ask some hard questions about what life is ultimately for. It requires a particular understanding of life's significance and meaning, an understanding in which reconciliation is not optional but the very fulfillment of all life.

How do we know if our living—the ways we set up our families and communities, run our politics and economies, grow food, use energy, educate our young and order our worship—is truly good or rightly lived? The Colossians hymn that I introduced in the first chapter speaks precisely to this line of questioning. It presents Jesus Christ as the key to what all life is about and what our living is ultimately for.

> He is the image of the invisible God, the firstborn of all creation; for in him all things in heaven and on earth were created, things visible and invisible, whether thrones or dominions or rulers or powers—all things have been created through him and for him. He himself is before all things, and in him all things hold together. He is the head of the body, the church; he is the beginning, the firstborn from the dead, so that he might come to have first place in everything. For in him the fullness of God was pleased to dwell, and through him God was pleased to reconcile to himself all things, whether on earth or in heaven, by making peace through the blood of his cross. (Col 1:15-20)

Jesus can show us what all life is for, because in him and through him all life comes to be in the first place. Christ is the one through whom all things are created (see 1 Cor 8:6), which means that he knows life's origin and end *from the inside.* Having the first place in everything, he also has authority over all creation (see Mk 4:35-41, in which Jesus calms the storm). With him, the world holds together. Without him, things fall apart into states of alienation, fragmentation and violence.

This is a peculiar way to speak about anyone, even for Christians! Many of us have been taught to look to Jesus as our

Savior. Not nearly as many have been taught to think of him as our *Creator*. What does this mean? Why does it matter?

It all starts with the affirmation that Jesus of Nazareth is the definitive, bodily manifestation of who God is. Jesus was not born merely to tell us a few things *about* God, things that will get us into some faraway heaven. No, Jesus *is* God. In his flesh the very "fullness" (*pleroma*) of God dwells. Touching his body, connecting to the way he moves through life and ministers to others, we can feel God's heavenly life realized on earth. He himself is the "image" (*eikon*) of the invisible God. Beholding him, we behold God. As the letter to the Hebrews puts it: "Long ago God spoke to our ancestors in many and various ways by the prophets, but in these last days he has spoken to us by a Son, whom he appointed heir of all things, through whom he also created the worlds. He is the reflection of God's glory and the exact imprint of God's very being, and he sustains all things by his powerful word" (Heb 1:1-3). In the words of the creeds, Jesus is "of one being with the Father" (Nicaea) and "truly God and truly man . . . of one substance with the father . . . and at the same time of one substance with us" (Chalcedon).

How the perfect uniting of Creator and creation could happen in a particular creature is an unfathomable mystery. Its implications, however, are immense and profound. For those who wonder why there is a world at all—as seventeenth-century philosopher G. W. Leibniz famously asked, "Why is there something rather than nothing?"—the beginnings of an answer are to be found by seeing how Jesus nurtures, heals, consoles, exorcises, reconciles and celebrates creatures. Jesus does all of these things out of a deep love for others, showing us that *all things are created so that they can experience and participate in the movements of love.* The experience and continuation of love is what living is ultimately for. Christ's love liberates and inspires others to experience life in its abundance and fullness. Seeing Jesus' devotion and concern for the world, we can say that the divine creation happens as an act of love and hospitality, in which God makes room for others to be themselves and flourish.

The incarnation means that our world does not exist as a random or pointless accident. Jesus showed us that the world exists so that love and life can grow together. As the Colossian hymn teaches us, to say that all things are created *in* and *through* and *for* Christ is also to say that God desires that every creature realize a complete life. Why? Because that is precisely what Jesus did in his ministries on earth. When Jesus encountered life's deformation, as he did when he saw hunger, illness, demon possession, discord and death, he showed love so that deformation could be turned to shared delight. When he found creatures on a path toward degradation and destruction, he turned them around so that they could enter paths of joy and shalom. Jesus made manifest in his own body that the life of love is what creation is for. Creation's purpose is definitively revealed in his self-sacrificial love.

We don't have to believe any of this. We can go on thinking that life is about individual fulfillment or getting power for ourselves while we can. We might insist that the path toward reconciliation is a dead end that only diminishes our prospects for fortune. Or we can become comfortably numb and resign ourselves to quiet desperation, in which we view the murders of people like Bill King as sad but to be expected. But in thinking this way, we also commit ourselves to a world in which division, suspicion, neglect, cutthroat competition and discord will inevitably be the outcome. It is precisely this sort of divided, broken and bleeding world that Jesus wants to redeem.

To understand Jesus properly, we have to appreciate how his living makes possible the transformation of our own. God became incarnate in Jesus Christ to show us and welcome us into what creaturely life is ultimately about and for. This means that salvation is not about being plucked out of creaturely life to some immaterial heaven beyond the world of creation. Salvation is about reconciling this creation so that it can know, taste and intimately experience God's heavenly life that is constantly making its way toward us. Looking to Jesus, we see heaven's earthly life realized.

Scripture makes clear again and again that God is Emmanuel, God with us. This is why God became incarnate in Jesus. This is why God sends the Holy Spirit to live within us as our animating and inspiring breath and to direct us in the ways of heavenly life. This is why Revelation shows us that the grand climax of God's cosmic drama has heaven *descend* to earth, because God's dwelling will forevermore be among mortals (see Rev 21:1-4). The goal is not our souls' escape from this world but the transformation of all creatures in their relationships with each other. The goal is that our embodied living radiates and becomes the perpetual expression of God's glory.

Another way to think about this is to reflect on John's description of Jesus as the "Word" (*Logos*) in whom we have life (see Jn 1:4). John's multiple references to abundant and true and eternal life indicate that it is possible to exist and not really be alive. As we all know, there are ways of existing that undermine and destroy life. To be fully and truly alive, we need to be grafted onto him like a branch to a vine (see Jn 15:4-5). Only then will our desire and will be in harmony with the Creator's desire for life. Jesus is the creating Word who was with God the Father in the beginning, and what Jesus is about is what God has always been about (see Jn 1:2 and Jn 15–17). Through him—through the forms of compassion and kindness he embodied—we see what creation looks like from God's point of view.

To understand John, we have to go back to the Genesis account of creation, which describes God as *speaking* order and harmony and beauty into the world. God says, for instance, "Let the earth put forth vegetation," and all kinds of plants with seed and fruit come to be (Gen 1:11). The detail about seed is not insignificant, because it is precisely through seed-bearing fruit that plants perpetuate themselves and feed the world. God's *Logos*, the speaking that God does, makes a world that is fertile and nutritious at the same time. It is the character of God's creativity that it establishes relationships—of fertility, nutrition and beauty—in which creatures can become fully alive.

Describing Jesus as the eternal Word is John's way of say-ing that we can look to him to find our way to a life that is full and abundant (see Jn 10:10). Why? Because his life and ministry embodied the kind of relationships that feed and heal and bring joy. Through his own being in the world, Jesus showed us what relationships in the world should look like. Because Jesus is the divine, creating Word, he is also the one who shows us how all creatures best *fit together* and relate to each other. He is like a cosmic conductor who holds the score that will lead all creatures into a harmonious and symphonic life—if we let him direct us. He wants us to listen to each other and to him, and then by becoming mutually attentive and sympathetic, produce a sound that is both melodic and a joy to hear. Living by this *Logos* means relating to each other in ways that nurture and strengthen relationships between crea-tures, so that all of us can experience Sabbath delight.

If Jesus is the divine, creating Word unleashing creation into its full potential, then insofar as we are *in* Christ or have the *mind* of Christ, we participate in God's renewing of cre-ation (see Phil 2:5). Paul made the point succinctly: "So if anyone is in Christ, there is a new creation: everything old has passed away; see, everything has become new" (2 Cor 5:17). As our Creator, Christ makes possible this new creation, which includes all creatures, and leads them into the fullness of life. With him nothing can remain the same or be engaged in old, familiar ways, because he shows us through his own life what life is meant to be. *Beholding Jesus, we not only see God; we see creation in an entirely new way.*

As disciples of Christ, we are no longer to regard anything from what Paul called "a human point of view" (2 Cor 5:16). This point of view assumes that the world's reason for being is to serve individual ambition and promote self-glorification. Others matter because of what they can do for me. But with Christ, all of this has changed. With Christ, we now see everything and everyone *through* him. He helps us realize that the world achieves fullness of life only when relationships between people and land and between people and each other are healthy and whole (see 2 Cor 5:18). To be *in* Christ means that we can no longer look at any creature in terms of political maneuvering, economic profitability or self-enhancement. If everything has become new because we now behold and engage it *through* him, then literally everything is wrapped within God's creating, healing, feeding and reconciling ways. In Christ every person is a child of God, and every created thing is God's gift to be protected, nurtured, shared and celebrated.

THE MINISTRY OF RECONCILIATION

Paul makes clear that the new creation that Christ makes possible is a gift. It is not something we can dream up or achieve through our own effort. We are too anxious and insecure or too arrogant and blind to even anticipate, let alone realize, the love that Christ's new creation presupposes. When we receive this gift of new life, however, we can participate in Christ's reconciliation of all things. "All this is from God, who reconciled us to himself through Christ, and has given us the ministry of reconciliation; that is, in Christ God was reconciling the world [*cosmos*] to himself, not counting their trespasses against them, and entrusting the message of reconciliation to us" (2 Cor 5:18-19).

What sort of ministry is this? The hymn in Colossians gives an answer few of us are eager to hear. It says that through Christ, God was pleased to reconcile to himself all things "by making peace through the blood of his cross" (Col 1:20). The ministry of reconciliation goes through a cross. It goes through blood!

To understand the significance of Christ's cross for the ministry of reconciliation, we can start by noting how the cross registered as a political symbol. In the Roman empire, crosses were a very public display and brutal reminder of imperial rule. The ancient Jewish historian Josephus referred to hanging on a cross as "the most wretched of deaths," because it caused a slow, excruciating death resulting from thirst, hunger, exposure and the trauma of multiple beatings. Jesus was put to death on a cross, indicating that he was perceived to be a serious threat to the *logos*, or order, by which the Romans secured their peace and prosperity.

When we think of the Roman empire today, it is easy to forget that it was made rich and vast through its brutality to others. We marvel at the immense public buildings and the engineering feats that transported water (via aqueducts) and grain (via fleets of ships) to Rome from places hundreds of miles away. But to grow the wheat to make the bread that would feed the home populations, small farmers around the Mediterranean were forcibly removed from their lands so that huge estates, called *latifundia*, could grow the commodities of grain or olive oil consumers back home wanted. Latifundia were the spoils of war made productive on the backs of slaves.

For a time, these latifundia were very productive. Because vast fields were consolidated and pressed into the production of a desired commodity, and because slaves were plentiful, shipload after shipload of grain could make its way to Rome's shores. This productivity, however, came at an exceptionally high human and ecological cost. Invaded peoples were kept "peaceful" by the constant threat and exhibition of brutality. Invaded lands were made productive through deforestation, the draining of wetlands and forms of agriculture that eroded and exhausted soil and choked waterways with silt. These are what we might call ecological forms of brutality. The Roman point of view (*logos*) and approach to land and people alike was strictly utilitarian: whatever exists is to be used to increase the wealth and glory of the Roman elite. Whatever gets in the way or might become a threat—such as a single man from Nazareth—must be eliminated.

Jesus *was* a threat to the Roman *logos*. He revealed the lie at the heart of the Pax Romana. He may not have been a direct or personal threat to the Roman emperor, but he stood as the decisive "No!" to the exploitation and violence that made Rome great. Jesus' life led to the nurture and healing and reconciling of creatures with each other. His ministry did not ever succeed through violent exploitation.

But Jesus was not only a threat to Rome. He continues to be a threat to all forms of economic and political order that promote peace and prosperity through abuse. Today he stands with sixty-four-year-old Sister Leonora Brunetto, a Roman Catholic nun, as she faces gunmen who want to kill her for her decades-long ministry of protecting the Amazon forest and its poor, landless workers from ranchers and foresters interested in a quick profit. He stood with Judy Bonds, a coalminer's daughter and peace activist who, despite death threats and personal assaults, spent her life defending the Appalachian Mountains and their people from Massey Energy Company, as it poisoned streams and blew up mountains.

Sister Leonora and Judy Bonds do not see the world according to what Paul called "a human point of view." Their imaginations have been captivated and inspired by the divine *Logos* that loves the world into life. When they look out, they see a glimmer of the new creation that Christ makes possible, a creation in which land and people flourish and in which peace is present. But they also know that their ministry of reconciliation requires that they put their energies, their gifts and even their lives on the line.

This leads us to a second insight as to why the ministry of reconciliation moves through a cross. Christ's cross is not only a symbol of Roman brutality; it is also a symbol of Christ's self-offering love given for the healing of creation. Recall that the Colossians hymn describes creation as "holding together" in Christ. Jesus holds things together—makes possible a symphonic life—because he introduces and embodies the love that creates harmony and conviviality rather than degradation and destruction. We could say that he unleashes a power that nurtures and enlivens others so that they can become all that God wants them to be. This power takes the form of loving service to others. As Paul puts it, Christ "emptied himself, taking the form of a slave, . . . he humbled himself and became obedient to the point of death—even death on a cross" (Phil 2:7-8). The cross reminds us that life in God is a life of *self-offering* service.

The service to which Christ invites us is not abstract or general. It begins with and continually returns to attentive regard for particular places and communities. Attention is crucial, because we cannot serve others properly—that is, in ways that benefit them instead of us—until we have taken time to appreciate their potential and their limits, their strengths and their needs. We need to look carefully for where the wounds are, and then learn from the wounded (and others who love them) regarding what will bring healing or relief.

The history of the civil rights struggle is instructive in this regard. The barriers that divided whites and blacks—which were responsible for so much misunderstanding, pain, violence and death—could not be overcome until whites and blacks committed to living side by side. Authentic reconciliation and community are not possible as long as groups of people view each other from a distance. We need to get close enough to see the pain we are causing each other and to listen carefully so that we can make the changes that will end unnecessary pain. Shared living makes possible the sympathy and the sensitivity we need in order to experience God's shalom and *Shabbat*.

Charles Sherrod, a field secretary of the Student Nonviolent Coordinating Committee, understood this when he said, "I have seen men share their bread till the last was gone. I have seen a band of ragged brothers willing to risk death for each other if need be. I have seen the strength of fellowship among those who formally refuse the fellowship of the church. Somehow I think this life must be shared for it to be comprehended; we do have something to offer but there is probably much to receive. This is an experiment in truth to find truth."

Reconciliation does not result from a top-down, mechanical or abstract process. It is a ministry and a gift that grows through bodily touch and practical life together. It is founded on a *Logos* that is real. It makes itself incarnate in relationships in which people spend enough time—even "waste time"—with each other so that they can delight in each others' joys and comfort each other in their pain.

When we appreciate that the divine *Logos* creates the whole world and not only people, we begin to see that the ministry of reconciliation will also extend to the land. Just as whites and blacks often live separate and segregated lives, so too have people developed forms of life that insulate them from the suffering and degradation of creatures and their homes. Reconciliation cannot happen as long as we see land abstractly or from a distance. We need to get close. We need to develop practical forms of life that bring us into clarifying and sympathetic relationship with soil, plant and animal life. Only then will we see the pain and destruction we are causing. By committing ourselves to a particular section of land and doing the hard labor such commitment requires, we learn the skills and habits that bring healing and life to it. This love and labor, which takes us deeply into the world, enables us to see the loveliness God creates there.

The proximity and training I have in mind are most clearly revealed in the work of gardening. Gardening is hard and daily labor that sharpens our understanding of the biophysical conditions that make fruit and flowers flourish. It is a form of attention that brings us into a sympathetic and nurturing relationship not only with pleasurable parts of our gardens— tulips and tomatoes, for example—but also with those elements that are less immediately attractive—worms and weeds. There is no substitute for this work if we desire to overcome the division and alienation that degrades the earth.

Gardening is also the form of work that best describes God's relationship to creation. God is not distant. God is the eternal Gardener on his knees, holding the soil of our lives in his hands, breathing life into it day after day (see Gen 2 and Ps 104). God is the eternal Farmer who comes with a bucket and hoe to water and weed his world so that there is a bountiful harvest. In God's reconciled world, "the hills gird themselves with joy, the meadows clothe themselves with flocks, the valleys deck themselves with grain, they shout and sing together for joy" (Ps 65:12-13). Participating with God in this gardening work helps us discover a joy that many of us would not think possible.

In 1958, Clarence Jordan delivered a sermon explaining why he had not yet left the bruised and battered land that is Koinonia Farm. He said:

Fifteen years ago we went there and bought that old run down eroded piece of land. It was sick. There were gashes in it. It was sore and bleeding. I don't know whether you've ever walked over a piece of ground that could almost cry out to you and say "Heal me, Heal me." I don't know if you feel the closeness to the soil that I do. But when you fill in those old gullies and terrace the fields and you begin to feel the springiness of the sod beneath your feet and you begin to feel that old land come to life and when you walk through a little old pine forest that you set out in little seedlings and now you see them reaching for the sky and you hear the wind through them; when you walk a little further over a bit of ground . . . and you go on over a hill where your children and all the many visitors have held picnics and you walk across a creek that you've bathed [in] the heat of summer, and men say to you "Why don't you sell it and move away?" they might as well ask, "Why don't you sell your mother." Somehow God has made us out of this old soil and we go back to it and we never lose its claim on us. It isn't a simple matter to leave it.

As our Creator, God is always close. In giving us the ministry of reconciliation through Christ, God invites us to become close to each other too, close enough both to see how we are wounding each other and to celebrate each other's triumphs.

Our culture does not encourage us to look for or get close to the wounds we inflict on each other and on the land. Nor does it equip us to understand how "normal" economic, political and social life creates wounds that need healing. But Christ does. Living with Christ, we are given the *Logos* to see a community like Cedar Grove and a field in southwest Georgia as part of Christ's new creation. We are inspired to turn land into a community garden that grows healthy food even as it repairs and nurtures the soil. We are compelled to gather around a table with people from all walks of life so that, through our eating, we discover community rather than alienation. With Christ, we create relationships in which the nurture of each other is paramount. In the offering of ourselves to each other, we give glory to God.

4

Field, Table, Communion

The Abundant Kingdom Versus the Abundant Mirage

FRED BAHNSON

One of my favorite stories from *The Sayings of the Desert Fathers* is the tale of John the Dwarf. One day John the Dwarf said to his elder brother, "I should like to be free of all care, like the angels, who do not work, but ceaselessly offer worship to God." John then shed his clothes and walked naked out into the desert. A week later he returned, sunburned and famished. John the Dwarf knocked on the door, but rather than opening the door his brother asked, "Who are you?" John said, "It is I, your brother." But his brother refused to open the door, saying, "John has become an angel and henceforth he is no longer among men." John the Dwarf begged to be let in but his brother refused, leaving him outside all night. In the morning, his brother opened the door. "You are a man," he said, "and you must once again work in order to eat." Whereupon John the Dwarf fell down on his face and asked his brother's forgiveness.

When it comes to food, I think most of us practice a kind of "John the Dwarf" spirituality. We wish to be "free of all care," which in our case is a sort of gnostic disdain for manual labor, soil husbandry, caring for physical places and living within our ecological limits. Some of us obsess over food and eat too much, while others starve our bodies. Some of us wish we had more to eat and go hungry. But for most of us, food is a given. It appears on the shelf almost magically, and we eaters give no thought to how it was grown or who had to work for substandard wages so that we can eat tomatoes in January. We wander in the desert of the industrial food system and let it feed us while we pursue higher, more angelic pursuits.

But even with a motive as pure as John the Dwarf's— ceaselessly offering worship to God—we must eventually end our naive sojourn in the desert of misguided intentions and come home. Our current food system, dependent as it is on the angelic gift of oil, has allowed us, for a brief window in human history, to believe that the work of growing food is somehow escapable. In agriculture, as in much of modern life, we have substituted oil and technology for people, and this has allowed us to erect an impressive scaffolding known as the food system. But as we will see in this chapter, that scaffolding is showing signs of collapse. Our bodies are collapsing, too. We have wanted "to be free of all care," yet soon we will need to go home and remember our first vocation: to serve and preserve the fertile soil (see Gen 2:15). We will need to learn how to live on the land in a way that witnesses not to our own hubris or technological know-how but to God's plenitude. We are men and women, not angels, and we must once again work in order to eat.

Because we are surrounded by a cornucopia of food, it is difficult to see any problem. Because less than one percent of us farm, we have no real understanding of how food is produced. All we know is that the modern food system has truly delivered. We have cheap food that arrives in a convenient manner. Yet *cheap* and *convenient* are questionable adjectives for a noun as important to our lives as food. If we look at the real costs, we begin to see a sight that appears troubling, even sinister.

We live amid two competing narratives. One is the abundant kingdom Jesus brought, where all receive enough and often there is abundance. The second narrative for most of us, however, is not scarcity but a more glamorous and alluring kind of abundance. I call it the *abundant mirage*. Nowhere are these two competing narratives more manifest than in the way we eat.

The demonic most often appears as a close shadow of the good, hard to distinguish until one looks closer. Inasmuch as our food system works against God's created order, poisoning bodies and landscapes, that system is demonic. It is a cruel parody of the way Jesus calls us to eat and live, and I believe it's one of the great forces at work against the kingdom of God, one of those systems Paul called the "principalities and powers," fallen and in need of redemption (Eph 6:12 NKJV). Before we look for the abundant life that Jesus invites us to inhabit, we must first unmask its demonic penumbra under whose darkness most of us now dwell.

THE ABUNDANT MIRAGE

Upon our family's return to the United States in 1987, after three years in Nigeria, my mother's most troubling moment was entering a grocery store. As she walked down the fluorescent aisles, with their gleaming array of endless food choices, she began to weep. She was overwhelmed. Everywhere she turned, there was so much food.

The thought of running out of food never crosses most of our minds. With such apparent abundance, how could it? The temptation with which we're faced is not between trusting God's abundance or being fearful of scarcity; rather, it is between competing narratives of plenty. We don't know what it means to feast at God's abundant table, because we have our faces buried in a feed trough. We're so accustomed to a cheap, continuous supply of food that we've come to mistake this for reality when really it is just a dream that we have manufactured for a while. We might call this dream *the abundant mirage.*

At first glance, this mirage is truly amazing. When we consider what it has given us, we have to be a little bit awestruck: mountains of vegetables year-round and endless choice of food so cheap that it claims only ten percent of our income, the least of any developed nation. In her book *Deeply Rooted: Unconventional Farmers in the Age of Agribusiness*, Lisa Hamilton profiles three farmers who once farmed conventionally and who have now switched to organic methods. Here is David

Podoll, a farmer from North Dakota, describing the conventional agriculture he once practiced: "If you take it from the standpoint of human labor efficiency, there is nothing more efficient than American agriculture. One person can combine $150,000 worth of corn in a day. One person! Holy smokes! It is a marvel, an absolute marvel of science that this can be done. When it comes to human labor, it is *the most* efficient agriculture the world has ever seen, by far. But from the standpoint of energy, there is nothing more *in*efficient. It is completely and absolutely, *irrevocably* unsustainable. It cannot endure past the oil age."

The key phrase here is the last: *it cannot endure past the oil age.* To maintain the abundant mirage requires a steady supply of cheap oil. It takes 7.3 calories of oil energy to produce one calorie of food. Another way to say it is that every bite we eat consumes seven times more of the earth's available energy than what we're receiving. We're eating our way into trouble. From the natural gas used to produce nitrogen fertilizer, to the diesel fuel needed for traction and shipping, our food is marinated in oil from farm to fork. As Podoll says, this is irrevocably unsustainable.

If oil ran out tomorrow, most of us would go hungry. In February 2010, I got to see firsthand a country where that very thing happened: Cuba. I traveled there with a group of agricultural researchers and spoke with a new generation of farmers who practice ecological farming. From them I learned about the great catastrophe that befell Cuba in the early 1990s.

Miguel Salcines Lopez is a farmer of the twenty-first century. With a stylish jean jacket and rakish cowboy hat adorning his six-foot frame, Miguel looks more like a Cuban John Wayne than a stooped, tired farmer. That's part of his game: he wants to make agriculture attractive, especially to the younger generation. Miguel is the president of Organopónico Vivero Alamar, Havana's largest and most successful organic garden. Actually, at eleven hectares (about twenty-seven acres), it's more of an urban farm than a garden. "In the past, agriculture in Cuba was demonized," Miguel told me. "People preferred to do anything but agriculture." But today, Cuban farmers—especially urban farmers—have become respected members of society, some earning three times as much as doctors.

Why the sudden shift from oil-based agriculture to ecological agriculture? *Necessity.* At one time, the Soviet Union was Cuba's main trading partner, supplying the island with not only meat and grains but also fertilizer, pesticides, tractors and oil—all the standard trappings of industrialized agriculture. But when the Soviet Union collapsed in 1991, Cuba was left scrambling to feed itself. Food disappeared from the shelves. Over the next three years, which Fidel Castro euphemistically dubbed "The Special Period in a Time of Peace," the average Cuban lost thirty pounds. Cubans learned how to grow food without all those fossil-fuel inputs because they had to. You could call it organic by default.

As Cuba demonstrates, our dependence on oil for food is a dangerous gamble. But the troubles don't stop there. Agricul-

ture also plays a decisively detrimental role in climate char
contributing one-third of all greenhouse gases. The livestock
industry alone produces 18 percent of all emissions. Creating
nitrogen fertilizers from natural gas, plowing the soil, trans-
porting and storing food: all these activities pump more carbon into the atmosphere.

Not everyone in the abundant mirage gets to eat; in chapter
six we will look at how the mirage perpetuates hunger and has
led to a global food crisis. In the United States, some people
suffer from hunger, but many more of us suffer from obesity.
Indeed, obesity is the flip side of the hunger coin. The number of hungry people in the world (one billion) has now been
equaled by the number of obese people, which means that
nearly one in three humans suffer from the ill effects of a poor
diet. Because so many of our calories now come from processed foods made from corn and soy, our obesity epidemic
has become one of our biggest health threats. And this comes
despite the plethora of health information available. Pablo
Monsivais, an assistant professor in the Department of Epide-
miology and the School of Public Health at the University of
Washington, says, "We know more than ever about the science of nutrition, and yet we have not yet been able to move
the needle on healthful eating."

But isn't the way we eat a matter of individual *choice*? Isn't
obesity, for example, just a lack of self-control? In his book
Stuffed and Starved: The Hidden Battle for the World Food System,
Raj Patel writes, "Every culture has had, in some form or
another, an understanding of our bodies as public ledgers on

which is written the catalogue of our private vices. The language of condemnation doesn't, however, help us understand why hunger, abundance and obesity are more compatible on our planet than they've ever been."

Patel's book challenges the assumption that food problems all boil down to a matter of individual consumer choice. It's not that people have become more gluttonous in the past fifty years; it's that the foods available to us have changed for the worse. Since the rise of industrial agriculture back in the 1940s, the nutrient content in commercially grown vegetables has steadily declined. A conventionally grown head of broccoli is no longer a head of broccoli, nutritionally speaking, but rather a green container for holding water. Add to that a sharp increase in the amount of fats, sugars and oils contained in processed foods, and you have a food supply that produces lots of *calories* but does not produce *health*.

The image we are given by the modern food system is the image of abundance, yet upon closer scrutiny we can see the falsity of such an image. It is an illusion we've been able to manufacture for a short time in human history and one that we can't sustain for much longer.

We might say that modern agriculture is at root a failure of speech. It is talk in which we deceive ourselves, and the truth is not in us. To boast of one hundred bushels-an-acre of wheat while our fields erode into the sea, and to proclaim that by 2050 the world's farmers must double production to feed a growing population while we waste as much food as it would take to feed those people: by such acts, we speak a lie. This is not the kind of abundance that reflects the kingdom of God. This is collectively sanctioned suicide.

From afar, a mirage looks enticing. But when you get closer, the image becomes distorted. Eventually the image disappears. The destruction this image causes, however, is no mirage.

Our food system is one of the powers and principalities, fallen and in need of redemption. Perhaps the way out of such a system is not to keep shoring up the old system or try to be reconciled to it, but to step around it and create something new. To create what might look less like a *system* and more like *a way of life*.

Something that might even begin to resemble the kingdom of God.

THE ABUNDANT KINGDOM

This is a book about reconciliation. The assumption with which Norman and I have proceeded is that reconciliation has too often been discussed in Christian circles as if it took place in a vacuum, as if only people and not trees, rivers, mountains and farms are swept up in God's redemptive drama. Our aim, then, is to point our attention back to the land, to say what a faithful life on it might look like, and to show that the land— indeed, the entire cosmos—is inextricably bound up in God's salvation through Jesus Christ (see Col 1:20).

In chapter two I told the story of the disciples on the road to Emmaus, how they only recognized Jesus when they sat down and broke bread with him. For the past two thousand years, Christians have sought our Lord Jesus in the breaking of the bread. Given that our myriad troubles with food begin with agriculture, perhaps it's time we extended our eucharistic imaginations to the fields and tables beyond the altar. Perhaps it is time we looked for our Lord also in the growing of the wheat.

"I came that they may have life," Jesus said, "and have it abundantly" (Jn 10:10). What kind of agriculture would make a space for the abundant kingdom of God to take root and flourish among us? This kingdom, I believe, is not an otherworldly place for which we must bide our time. Nor is it a purely inward experience. It is an actual social reality, visible whenever God inspires people to live it out. And yet seeing it requires training.

Susan Sides, garden manager for The Lord's Acre, a community garden in North Carolina, puts it this way: "The garden, like the kingdom of God, consists mostly of the invisible and is infinitely complex, exactly why it's so hard to explain or define. The work we're called to do here at The Lord's Acre is as small as dust and as large as the mind and heart of God. It is humbling, mysterious, and joyful. We don't own it, create it or control it. We certainly don't sustain it. In our work, we try to mirror the kingdom."

The Lord's Acre began in 2009 when people from several churches worked with community leaders in Fairview, North Carolina, to provide fresh, organic produce to local food banks. In their first year alone, thanks to the considerable gardening skills of Susan Sides, a lifelong organic gardener who uses intensive and sustainable production methods, they were able to raise three tons of vegetables on a mere quarter acre. We need not rely on chemicals or fossil fuels to create abundance, as The Lord's Acre demonstrates.

The question of *how* to practice agriculture in the abundant kingdom needs to be clarified, and to that we will soon turn. First we must ask what Christianity has to teach us about growing food. Jesus offered no explicitly agrarian advice, although mention of food and farming abounds in his parables and metaphors. There is no biblical roadmap or set of rules for practicing a just and sustainable agriculture; that's not how Scripture works. But perhaps we can start with the via negativa: if abundance is predicated on the destruction of ecosystems, creatures and human bodies, as the vast majority of agriculture currently is, then it's not just a shoddy kind of abundance. It is collective thievery.

Perhaps thinking about growing food in a way that welcomes the kingdom of God should begin with Jesus' command in the Sermon on the Mount: "strive first for the kingdom of God and his righteousness, and all these things will be given to you as well" (Mt 6:33). It's noteworthy that Jesus' command comes after a long passage in which he lays out a *modus operandi* for living, a sort of kingdom economics. You can't worship both God and mammon, he says. In place of *mammon* we can also substitute *modern agriculture*; both compete with God for our trust. Both claim to take care of all our needs.

Jesus next describes the alternative. "Therefore I tell you," Jesus says, "do not worry about your life, what you will eat or what you will drink" (Mt 6:25). He points to the birds of the air as examples of such a worry-free existence. At first glance, it would seem that Jesus is advocating a kind of John-the-Dwarf approach to life, traipsing about in merry oblivion while the American food system feeds us. But that's not what Jesus is saying. Rather, he is trying to get his followers to relax their grip, give up their illusion of control, leave the abundant mirage and live instead in the abundant kingdom he has brought. When one trusts in God's abundance, sometimes twelve baskets will remain, sometimes seven, and sometimes nothing will be left. But there will always be enough.

Being free from worry about what we will eat or drink is not a call to laziness. As Wendell Berry put it, "When we pray that terrible prayer, *Thy kingdom come, thy will be done, on earth as it is in heaven*, then we can't withhold our work." Rather, Jesus' admonishment is simply a call to give up control over our daily sustenance. Food is not a product. It is not "fuel for the machine." It is not a commodity or a reflection of our technological ingenuity. It is before everything else an unearned gift from God, manna from heaven, a blessing. As eaters in the abundant mirage, which offers the illusion of control and limitless bounty, we need to learn how to receive food as a gift and not a given. Perhaps a more kingdom-centered approach to eating begins with the radical trust that God's abundance is enough. We don't need to worry. Everyone can eat their fill. Such a life, Walter Brueggemann writes, is "grounded in *creation faith*, in the conviction that the world is God's creation that is designed to exhibit and enact God's good will for the abundant life." And that should lead us to what Brueggemann calls "astonished gratitude."

To receive food as a gift is going to mean walking away from the mirage. The church must use her eucharistic imagination to create a new paradigm of agriculture. We need an infrastructure that models Jesus' abundant kingdom. What if we abandon the centralized food economy and instead create new food communities centered on the local practice of growing healthy food together? And what if we then invite the hungry to the feast? If we do, then our way of life will appear quite different from the illusory substitute to which we've become accustomed. And if we're to welcome God's abundant kingdom, it should be visible both in our fields and at our tables.

THE FIELD: CONSIDER THE LILIES, HOW THEY GROW

Our fields speak a language, which, as the psalmist tells us, is a language of praise (see Ps 19:1-4). Instead of the language of industrialization, which is the language of efficiency and control, we should learn to speak the language of praise. And that means a move toward agricultural practices that exhibit what Liberty Hyde Bailey, in his 1915 book *The Holy Earth* called *earth righteousness*.

I said earlier that Jesus didn't have any explicitly agrarian advice, but perhaps there's one exception. Jesus told his disciples in the Sermon on the Mount not to worry, then added something that provides an imaginative leaping point for much of what I wish to say below. "Consider the lilies of the field, how they grow," he said, "they neither toil nor spin, yet I tell you, even Solomon in all his glory was not clothed like one of these" (Mt 6:28-29). Jesus used this example about clothing, and why his disciples shouldn't worry about what they wear, but I take his words here also to be a kind of agrarian directive: *consider the lilies, how they grow. Look at the created order God has established. You will never do better than this. So trust in this order and imitate it.* Neither Solomon in all his glory—nor, we might add, Monsanto or Archer Daniels Midland or Cargill and their fertilizers or pesticides or genetically modified seeds—can out-create what God has created.

For ten thousand years we have tried to outdo creation in our attempt to grow food, trusting in our own ingenuity. We have mostly failed. Modern agriculture is a zero-sum game in which we steadily, as Wes Jackson says, "contribute to the drawdown of the capital stock of the planet." Yet it need not be. Indeed, as Jackson and other practitioners of the consider-the-lilies approach—an approach I will call *regenerative agriculture*—tell us, we can use nature as analog rather than antagonist. *Consider the lilies of the field* turns out to be sound agriculture advice.

Around the world there is a growing movement among agriculturalists to look to nature as a model for how to practice agriculture. Wes Jackson and his fellow plant breeders at The Land Institute, which Norman will describe later in the book, are some of the biggest proponents of this practice—what poet Alexander Pope called "consulting the genius of the place."

But there are others. Instead of imposing our own agricultural scheme, most often monocultures of annual crops, we should look at how lilies grow. They don't grow in monocultures, but in polycultures; that is, they grow mixed with other plants. Some of those plants fix nitrogen, fertilizing their neighbors. Lilies don't need someone to plant them every year; they are perennial. Our monocultures of annual crops exact a heavy toll on the land; if we're to practice agriculture in a way that conserves life rather than degrades it, we will need to depend much more on perennial polycultures for our food supply.

Yet we still must eat annual crops, and forms of agriculture such as biointensive mini-farming use God's creation as a model for such crops. Using conventional agricultural practices, it takes just over an acre of land to feed one person in the United States for a year, and far more energy and topsoil are wasted than are produced in food calories. Using biointensive methods, you can feed ten people for a whole year on that one acre, and you can build soil fertility while doing it. That same acre, by the way, would feed one cow for a whole year, or it would fill up the gas tank of your car with ethanol exactly *twice*.

The list of other types of regenerative agriculture is long: permaculture, biodynamic agriculture, agroforestry, Farming God's Way, Fukuoka no-till farming, and rotational grazing livestock systems, among others. In the sustainable agriculture world, some of these names can become mirages of their own, a territory to be policed and defended by practitioners as *the* answer. But we need not get too hung up on names or programs, and no one system need dominate; food growers in the abundant kingdom can learn from all of these bodies of knowledge. The underlying idea to remember is that the ecosystems in which we find ourselves—created by God and deemed "very good"—are far more adept at growing things than we are. Making ourselves students of those ecosystems is what it means to serve and preserve the fertile soil God entrusted to our care (see Gen 2:15). Our role is not to outdo creation or copy it verbatim, but to use it as an analog, a controlling metaphor, for how we tend our own fields.

The encouraging news is that while the abundant mirage destroys our soil base, the consider-the-lilies approach to agriculture restores it, while feeding people in the process. Here's one example from one of the most difficult food-growing regions in the world: the Sahel in Niger.

Before humans started growing their monocultures there, the ecological pattern in the Sahel was savannah. Trees were prevalent until high deforestation rates and the burning of organic matter led to severe environmental degradation, which left soils lifeless and exposed to erosion. This resulted in poor crop yields, which led to high rates of malnutrition and extreme poverty. With 90 percent of its population being farmers or herders dependent on a beleaguered landscape, Niger is one of the poorest countries in the world.

Last year I corresponded with Australian agricultural missionary Peter Cunningham, who worked for ten years in the Sahel desert of Niger. One of the ongoing problems in Niger is farmers' dependence on monocultures—a dependence that, Peter said, "should have been done away with a long time ago." Single-crop solutions, including the genetically modified drought-tolerant maize developed for Africa by Monsanto, don't work. They are not robust enough to withstand Sahel's environmental stresses.

The answer, Peter and his counterparts in Niger discovered, is a holistic approach based on the Sahel's original ecosystem. "In zones where God created the ecosystem as a savannah—trees, grasses and herbs—we should follow that pattern with trees," Peter told me. "If large areas of productive land once had trees and were cleared, we should go back to having trees with annual crops planted between them."

Following the pattern with trees was an idea Peter and local Niger farmers developed into an agroforestry project they call Sowing Seeds of Change in the Sahel. In addition to indigenous trees, the project featured edible acacia trees from Australia. The acacias, which add nitrogen to the soil, serve to "nurse" annual crops and other trees, which are planted in alleys in between. Both people and livestock can eat their seeds, which are high in protein. Acacias confirm the Hausa proverb: *the one who plants trees will never be hungry.*

Acacias have long been known for their benefits. Peter pointed out to me that in Isaiah 41:18-19, God says, "I will make the wilderness a pool of water, and the dry land springs of water. I will put in the wilderness the cedar, the acacia, the myrtle, and the olive." Apparently Isaiah was channeling some divine agroforestry advice; as a nitrogen-fixing tree, the acacia feeds the soil and other trees around it. Where acacias are planted, springs of water follow, if not visible to the eye then at least present in the soil.

Because the Niger farmers are now following creation's pattern of kingdom abundance, soil fertility is increasing. Degraded lands are healing. Farmers are feeding themselves in good years and in drought years. As more Sahelian farmers employ these methods, Peter believes, they could even begin to reverse desertification and create food-secure oases across the Sahel. That's no mirage. Imagine it, as did the prophet Isaiah: a once-dry land now full of acacias and springs of water.

Most of us don't live in a savannah-like ecosystem. Yet wherever we live, the local ecosystem is waiting for us to learn from it and to mimic its abundance in producing our own. If we live in the Midwest, our agricultural analog is the prairie; if we live in the eastern United States, it's the deciduous forest. In the case of the latter, we can build edible forest gardens, perennial polycultures that can produce all of our fruit, nuts and vegetables. As oil grows increasingly scarce and expensive, all those trucks laden with fruit and nuts from California's Central Valley can't keep coming forever. Why not begin growing our own and sharing the abundance with our neighbors?

With our own food forests, we need not hide under our beds when we hear phrases like *debt ceiling* or *double-dip recession*. We can withdraw our trust from giant financial institutions, which we have learned are not "too big to fail," and place our trust instead in a God who will provide enough for everyone. We need not spend our energy protesting the abundant mirage or seeking its downfall, since its downfall is inherent in its very nature as one of the powers and principalities in rebellion against God. The church should put her energy, therefore, into creating alternative economies. *Consider the lilies of the field, how they grow.* If Jesus Christ is the one in whom the world holds together, as Colossians 1:17 suggests, then regenerative agriculture is a way to learn in small and localized ways *how* the world hangs together and to then plant our fields according to that reality.

People like Peter Cunningham and his friends in Niger demonstrate that considering the lilies makes good practical sense; it works far better than modern agriculture's mirage, though it is more difficult. In that sense, it would be wise to consider the lilies of the field and how they grow well in advance of the day that the mirage will vanish and leave us scrambling for food like the Cubans in the early 1990s. Regenerative agriculture is a good to be pursued in itself, yet it is not an end in itself. It is a means by which we can seek first the kingdom of God.

The abundant mirage substitutes fossil fuels and cheap labor for human intelligence and honest labor, and burns seven times more energy than it gives. Before that mirage vanishes and leaves us outside the door hungry and cold, we should change course. An agriculture that considers the lilies is not a throwback to loincloths and spear-chucking, although it will require sacrifices, as well as many more people returning to farming. Florida tomatoes in January and Argentinian apples in March come to mind as luxuries that will not be feasible in a sunshine-powered world. Yet we can create gardens and farms that give us enough or even more than we need and that contribute to the resilience and health of our ecosystems. A slightly shriveled Stayman Winesap apple that overwintered in the root cellar is still far tastier than a South American Gala any day. Churches, with their land and resources, can encourage such local examples of God's abundant fields.

THE TABLE: FROM *ALIMENTO* TO *COMIDA*

Not everyone in the abundant kingdom needs to learn the art of gardening or farming, although as oil becomes scarce, many more will need to. But everyone needs to eat. Our table fellowship needs to be extended to include the fields and how our food is grown, and it needs to be extended to include those who hunger.

Food is a matter of justice. Following the example of our Lord, any food practice in the abundant kingdom must offer the outcast and marginalized seats of honor. Jesus told us that when we feed the hungry, we're really feeding him. Yet we've turned that ancient practice into the spiritually tepid "food drive," in which we're encouraged to rifle through our pantries and pull out those unpalatable cans of Chef Boyardee or Campbell's tomato soup for the poor. Jesus deserves better than the rejects of the abundant mirage.

Instead, why not do something extravagant? Why not throw Jesus a grand feast every week, like John Crognale does at the Welcome Table in Black Mountain, North Carolina? John once owned a five-star restaurant in Monterey, California.

Since moving to Black Mountain, he decided to start using his chef skills to feed the hungry. Each Wednesday at St. James Episcopal Church in downtown Black Mountain, John and his assistants serve up a high-quality meal, using fresh and often local organic ingredients. Susan Sides and The Lord's Acre have supplied many of the vegetables.

At the Welcome Table, there is no sign among the volunteers of dour-faced charity or somber "Christian duty." These folks are enjoying themselves. John Crognale, attired in his crisp white chef's jacket and setting out the finest of feasts for his guests, exemplifies the gracious host. Here everyone is treated as if they were not homeless people in need of a shower but patrons of the finest restaurant. They are treated, in other words, like dignified human beings deserving of the best food available. Anyone is welcome, as the Welcome Table's motto states: "Whosoever will, may come."

That's the abundant kingdom made visible. Why feed Jesus the dregs of the abundant mirage—high-fructose corn syrup, white bread, Jell-O, canned corn—when we could offer him fresh, organic vegetables? The abundant table, fed by the abundant fields surrounding it, is one of the loveliest forms of witness the church can make. As one of The Lord's Acre garden interns told Susan Sides, "This garden makes social justice beautiful." Instead of being *against* the poverty and hunger that the abundant mirage produces, why not be *for* something much more inviting?

A few years ago, my Brazilian friend Claudio Oliver and a group of his friends were so attracted to the vision of God's abundance that they had read about in Scripture that they decided to go for it. Several of them quit their jobs and began an experiment in kingdom-centered community in Curitiba, Brazil. They called it *Casa da Videira*, which means "Home of the Vine," and described it as "a cooperative of families that have decided to create a vibrant, sustainable place in which to live a balanced, relationally-focused life, caring for God's creation and inspiring the people around them." What that looks like might best be called *abundant kingdom homesteading*. They are involved in urban food production, both gardening and with animals. They make and sell soap from recycled vegetable oil. It has been financially difficult for them to completely leave the abundant mirage, and some of them still work in traditional jobs. Making an income is a constant struggle. Yet it's also clear that they have found much joy to share in this kingdom experiment. "We understand that we can't think about food without referring to the narrative of creation and linking it with a deep understanding of how we have been created to be the bearers of the Spirit and part of the community of life on this planet, not its owners," Claudio said.

They try to make eating an act within the cycle of life, not simply as an act of consumption. For the folks at Casa da Videira, that means turning their attention to the dejected and rejected—the leftovers. As Christians living in the city, their main concern is how the relationship with food in the city reveals our neglect of creation. "Every day," says Claudio, "tons of nutrients arrive, are delivered, cooked in the city and more than 30 percent of it is wasted." So each day, Claudio and his friends collect some of that food waste. Within a two-mile radius from their home, they collect vegetable scraps from grocery stores; food scraps and leftovers from neighbors; lawn clippings, wood chips and leaves from the curb; and coffee grounds from coffee shops. This is usually three to four tons of organic garbage a month—the refuse of roughly 150 households. They then compost it all in a backyard measuring less than a tenth of an acre, turning it into beautiful soil.

They raise fifteen different heirloom varieties of chickens, who, Claudio says, "help us remember the variety of creation," and who eat as they did "in grandma's time"—feasting on food scraps, greens, corn and worms provided by the composting program. Feeding the chickens worms for protein means that they don't have to feed them soybeans, which is one of Brazil's most destructive monocrops. Sixty-eight percent of Brazil's crops, including soybeans, are now genetically modified, so choosing not to use soy is a small act of resistance against the abundant mirage. The wood chips are used for the chickens' bedding, and the chickens provide them with a good number of eggs every day. The roosters get eaten when they start "singing." Four goats provide milk and cheese when they are in kid season, and the thirty rabbits are a major source of the community's meat. The goats' and rabbits' urine and manure become part of the compost mix. This whole nutrient cycle ends in their lasagna garden bed, where they produce around three tons of organic vegetables per year for themselves and their neighbors.

But food production is only part of community life at Casa

da Videira. Every day three or four families have one meal together: two university teachers, two homemakers, one doctor, children and friends have what Claudio calls "a happy meal (the real one)" every day, sometimes with more than eighteen different vegetables.

In Portuguese, Claudio explains, there are two terms for food: *comida* and *alimento*. "I always say, *alimento* is what McDonald's and nutritionism gives to you, *comida* is what your mum makes for you." *Alimento* is the amount of daily nutrients you need to stay on your feet, "where you work like a chicken in an 'egg factory' in order to make money to buy more *alimento*." *Comida*, though, is what we might call "soul food." Here's how Claudio describes the complex goodness that happens around *comida*: "It's a family together, people talking, warm fresh veggies, sweet potatoes with brown sugar and cinnamon in the morning (for Southerners in your country), corn bread, laughing, crying, prayer, thanksgiving, culture, old histories, yesterday morning histories, little ones learning who we are through food, love, fights, reconciliation, dating, a baby's first meal, planning next lunch or tomorrow's dinner. This one hour of *life* is about remembering who and *whose* we are, from where we come, memories to help us cross difficult times with hope. . . . well . . . this is *comida*."

At Casa da Videira, daily practice is based on the promise in John 10:10: "I came that they may have life, and have it abundantly." Claudio refers to the Greek word *zoe*, which comes from *zao*, and means "I live" or "I am alive."

Zoe is what it's like to feel alive. So we understand that what Jesus offers for us is this sensation of being alive, enjoying life, living abundantly. All this starts when we look to those pieces of life, sent to die as garbage, and reintroduce them into the cycle of life, respecting them as part of creation. It's a process that begins in the soil and ends at our tables. We harvest our veggies from this cycle, we breed our animals inside of it, we even kill them (the kosher way because we don't want them being treated as commodities but as someone that gives their lives for us to stay alive). Where the world sees garbage, we see nourishment; where the world sees death, we see life; in a world of loneliness, we discover community.

THE COMMUNION: CREATING INFRASTRUCTURES OF HOLINESS

When God's kingdom comes, on earth as in heaven, it comes in smallness and obscurity to a world mostly ignorant of its power. We've settled for a paltry vision of an earthly life whose main purpose is to serve as a holding tank for the next. Meanwhile, Jesus' kingdom is on the move. What is the *telos* of our existence if not aligning our lives with that coming reality? Perhaps we can't see God's kingdom among us because the patterns and places of our daily lives prevent such vision. We need places that can restore our sight.

As the Cuba example demonstrates, it will require a massive transition away from fossil fuels—fuels that seem to cause us so much trouble. Think tanks like the Post-Carbon Institute and Transition US—which estimate the "peak time" for oil extraction before supplies begin to dwindle—are predicting a steady decline instead of a rapid freefall like the Cuban experience. But even with a gradual descent, this much is clear: relying on oil to feed us is clinging, like John the Dwarf, to an angelic and carefree existence not grounded in reality.

The language of transition is hopeful because it leads to practical steps. A movement called Transition Towns started in England about five years ago. Instead of waiting around for sweeping legislation, little towns around England decided to try to wean themselves from fossil fuels and create alternative food economies on their own. They pooled their funds to buy solar panels for the block. They started community gardens and orchards, built bike paths, created a local currency and started community kitchens where people could preserve food. All were attempts to extract themselves from the global economy as quickly and completely as they could. The Transition Town movement is only about four years old, and already it is moving across the globe. There is a small but growing Transition movement in the United States. I like the Transition Town movement because it frames our problems hopefully. It took an immense amount of creativity to create the fossil-fuel-dependent world, say the Transition folks, and we can apply that same creativity to cushioning our descent on the way down.

In the years ahead, I believe that the church will need computer programmers and lawyers and economists to direct their creativity toward things like permaculture, biointensive gardening and natural systems agriculture. In a world of diminishing fossil fuels, climate disruption, sick bodies and eroding topsoil, a lot more of us are going to need to put our minds and shovels to work learning how to feed ourselves and our neighbors. Here is where our John the Dwarf analogy breaks down: too few of us have a "big brother" to go home to, someone who can feed us when our angelic detour in the abundant mirage leaves us cold and hungry and begging to be let in.

The picture before us is only bleak if we insist that the scaffolding of the abundant mirage will somehow hold. We need the mind of Christ to transfer our hope away from that shaky structure and return it to our firm foundation, the One who has become the chief cornerstone, the One whose yoke is easy and whose burden is light, the One in whom all things were created and deemed "very good." We need only imagine the abundant way of life our Lord invites us into and then begin living as if that were true.

What if our homes and churches went from being primarily sites of *consumption* to places of *production*, as the scholar and priest Ivan Illich suggested? What if we planted church-supported community gardens, permaculture parishes, Transition churches, and apostolic farms that fed entire neighborhoods? What if seminaries trained every future pastor in the agrarian arts, ecological literacy and sunshine-powered living? What if church lawns stopped being dumping grounds for pesticides and petro-fertilizers and started growing zucchini and heirloom tomatoes for the local homeless shelter? What if bishops and deacons and divinity school deans—and even the local church finance committee—took the church's money out of the abundant mirage and put it into the much saner, more lasting savings account called soil fertility? What if we created *infrastructures of holiness*, where God's kingdom of shalom could flourish on earth as in heaven?

Everything I've been saying comes down to this unasked question: how much shalom can we expect to see this side of the eschaton? I don't have the answer. I do know that, living as we do in the abundant mirage, we haven't expected nearly enough.

These soil-tenders I've described, people like Susan Sides and Peter Cunningham and Claudio Oliver, have expected God's abundant kingdom because they have been looking for it. They have tried to live it, and in living as if the abundant kingdom were real, they have been given a glimpse. They've seen God's shalom caress their land like a lover caressing his beloved's cheek. What they've seen has been fragile and small and mostly hidden, not something that easily fits on a goals-and-outcomes report or a press release or a Twitter feed. That's because God's shalom is a wily and mysterious creature, shy and elusive around the world's probing gaze, but one that lifts its head whenever we treat the land and those who dwell on it with care.

I remember the times at Anathoth Community Garden when we shared the Eucharist amid collards and kohlrabi. Heaven came down to earth on those Saturday mornings, and

I carry those memories with me like a pearl of great price. These moments await all of us whenever we blur the lines between field, table and Eucharist.

My prayer for the church is that we will stretch our eucharistic imaginations and see that the sacrament of Christ's body and blood doesn't end at the altar. God's communion spreads outward into the fields, the creeks and rivers, the gardens and farms which feed us, out to the stranger on the road and back again to the lifted elements. Had we the "conviction of things not seen," we would recognize this seamless flow of nutrients both visible and invisible, profane and holy (Heb 11:1). And we would be changed.

5

Reconciliation Through Eating

NORMAN WIRZBA

*I*n what are surely some of the most succinct expressions of God's transforming presence, the Gospels tell us that Jesus was known (and despised by religious leaders) as the fellow who "welcomes sinners and eats with them" (Lk 15:2). Although John the Baptist ate no bread and drank no wine, Jesus was the Son of Man who came eating and drinking, prompting people to say, "Look, a glutton and a drunkard, a friend of tax collectors and sinners!" (Lk 7:34; Mt 11:19). The kingdom of God is a place where people come from the east and the west, from the north and the south, and eat (see Lk 13:29). In the New Jerusalem, the place where we will live eternally with the God who has chosen to dwell with us, people from all the nations will gather around the tree of life to be healed and fed by its fruit (see Rev 22:1-2).

That eating mattered to Jesus should not surprise us if we understand that eating is the daily enactment of our dependence on other people, the land and ultimately God. Every time we take a bite, we bear witness to a bewildering array of relationships that connect us to earthworms, raspberry shoots, water, sunshine, farmers, cooks and friends. When we eat well, these relationships are honored and nurtured. When we eat poorly, we demean and degrade the sources of nourishment that make living a possible feast. Jesus cares about eating because it is in the growing, preparing and sharing of food that we bear witness to God's desire that all creatures taste life fully.

It is easy for many people, especially when walking through a well-stocked grocery store with its attractive displays, to take eating for granted and to assume that food is of little significance for Christian faith and life. We might recall Matthew's Gospel, in which Jesus says, "[D]o not worry about your life, what you will eat or what you will drink, or about your body, what you will wear. Is not life more than food, and the body more than clothing?" (Mt 6:25). God knows that we need to eat. Our task is not to worry but to trust that God will provide.

Although we should certainly care about the fact that well over a billion people still do not have enough to eat, it is tempting to assume that this distinctly Christian concern about eating ends when food has been adequately distributed and shared. This is a serious mistake. Jesus' admonition is directed to the ways in which worry dominates and distorts our relationships with the world and each other. Clearly life *is* more than food. We can, if we are not careful, turn eating into an idolatrous affair by making food our obsessive focus. But there is no life without food. God created a world in which every creature lives by eating. God daily sustains creatures by providing them with gifts of decomposition, photosynthesis and digestion, which are essential for the eating we enjoy. On the first Sabbath sunrise, God looked out on the world and pronounced it good. Seeing the creatures eat, he also made it delectable. That Jesus ate with sinners is both a practical and a profound action because it shows us how God relates to us, how we are to relate to each other and how we need to relate to the food itself. When our relationships in these three areas are properly configured, creation is nurtured and reconciled, God is glorified and heaven is tasted.

Appreciating the Christian significance of eating is difficult because for many of us, food has been reduced to a commodity. It has become a product much like any other, which means that our thinking about it centers on questions of availability, brand, convenience and price. When we consider how many "foods" now come wrapped in a highly stylized marketing plan, it is difficult to see past all the contrivance and find the hands of God. If we eat one of the many varieties of Doritos® tortilla chips, for instance, we are told that "a powerful crunch that unlocks . . . bold and unique flavors" will give us "immersive and memorable experiences." When we learn that many foods are making us fat and sick—rates of obesity, cholesterol, diabetes, acid reflux, hypertension, anorexia, heart disease and cancer are all on the rise—we might think that eating is a dangerous affair that, if we are not careful, can kill us.

Scripture does not present food to us as a product or enemy. Instead, as in this passage from Psalm 104, it describes food and drink as God's precious gifts, given for the health and enjoyment of all creatures.

You make springs gush forth in the valleys;
    they flow between the hills,
giving drink to every wild animal;
    the wild asses quench their thirst.
By the streams the birds of the air have their habitation;
    they sing among the branches.
From your lofty abode you water the mountains;
    the earth is satisfied with the fruit of your work.
You cause the grass to grow for the cattle,
    and plants for people to use,
to bring forth food from the earth,
    and wine to gladden the human heart,
oil to make the face shine,
    and bread to strengthen the human heart. . . .
O LORD, how manifold are your works!
    In wisdom you have made them all;
    the earth is full of your creatures. . . .
These all look to you to give them their food in due
        season;
    when you give to them, they gather it up;
    when you open your hand, they are filled with good
        things.
(Ps 104:10-15, 24, 27-28)

To believe that God created the world as an act of love is also to believe that potatoes, apples, milk and cheese are God's love made touchable, fragrant and delicious. To be faithful to this hospitable God is to participate in and extend the divine hospitality that welcomes, nurtures and delights in the world.

FOOD SHAME

It had been another tough day. When Matthew arrived at his office, he opened an email that turned his day upside down. Thinking he was going to put the finishing touches on an overdue report, he instead discovered that a branch office was in crisis mode. He spent the day putting out fires he didn't start.

Matthew was supposed to be home by four so that he could prepare dinner for the kids before the night's soccer practice. That didn't happen. Running late, he entered the drive-thru and picked up an order of chicken nuggets, fries, chocolate milk and apple wedges. They all ate in the car on the way to the practice field. His wife was not happy to see the fast-food bags—again. But she is really busy too. In his defense, Matthew showed her the uneaten apples as a sign that he was trying to make the best of the situation.

This scenario is hardly atypical. America has been dubbed the "fast food nation" because relatively few of us have the time to make good eating a priority. Drive-thrus at the many fast-food chains have a steady stream of vehicles. Grocery-store managers who order tens of thousands of different food products know that convenience is a high priority for consumers, so they stock multiple kinds of prepared and processed items—"foods" that can be prepared quickly with the push of a microwave button. Dining room tables are stacked with stuff rather than meals, because very often we have to eat on the run, at the desk or in a car.

Time isn't the only major factor shaping the way our nation eats. The other is cost. Although we expect serving sizes to be large, we also expect the price to be cheap. Owing to the distortions of our industrial food system, it is often cheaper to buy a hamburger than a head of broccoli, a bottle of soda than water. All our cheap food, however, comes at a very high price. The cheap sticker price at the store does not reflect the costs associated with herbicide- and fertilizer-laden soils, poisoned and depleted waters, the burning of vast quantities of fossil fuels, abused animals, abused farmworkers, poorly treated and compensated food-service providers and the myriad diet-related diseases that are causing healthcare costs to skyrocket. Our demand for cheap food is slowly degrading and destroying all life on our planet. The generation demanding it, however, actually spends the smallest percent of income on food that the world has ever known.

A lot of this convenient, cheap food tastes pretty good. Sodium, sugars, fats and artificial flavorings have been generously added to give us a temporarily satisfied feeling. But if we could get behind the slick packaging and enticing presentation, we would discover that we have much to be ashamed about. To be *ashamed* means that we know we have done wrong before another. It means that we have not treated others in a way that honors their integrity.

But many of us are not ashamed about our eating. We are not in a position or we do not take the time to learn how our desire for convenience and cheapness is so destructive of the sources of life. Today's average eater is likely the most ignorant eater in history. How many of us grow any food at all? Relatively few people know where their food comes from or understand the conditions necessary for it to be safely, sustainably and nutritiously produced. Our food industry doesn't want you to know.

I regularly teach a class on eating and the life of faith. At the opening of each class, I ask a student to give a short report on a favorite food. I ask them to research where the food comes from and how it is produced and marketed, and to assess its nutritional value. Almost without fail they begin their presentations by saying, "Well, I won't be eating this anymore!" They also report on how difficult it was for them to learn about the food. When companies are called, they rarely give straight or helpful answers. Websites are full of misinformation. Food companies don't want you to understand the food. They want you to think that eating their product is fun or sexy or performance-enhancing. Think about the ever-popular and even iconic Twinkie, one of America's best-loved snack cakes: President Clinton put one in a time capsule! What's it doing in our stomachs?

The shame of our eating becomes clearer when we consider the chicken nugget that millions of children like to eat. To get on a kid's meal menu, it has to be cheap. To make it cheap, the chicken-producer has to be paid the smallest amount possible. To raise chicken most efficiently, the chicken-producer has to find ways to get more chickens into his or her barns and then get them to butcher weight as quickly as possible. To do that, it is best to genetically alter chickens so that their breasts become huge really fast, since Americans crave white meat. Today's engineered, confined chicken reaches full size in nearly half the time of traditional breeds. The enhanced breasts of these birds become so burdensome that many chickens' legs break under their own crushing weight. It is also important that their diets be supplemented by antibiotics, because crammed chicken houses are breeding grounds for disease. Room for the chickens to roam is not critical, since their breasts are so large that walking is difficult. Small spaces also make it easier for them to be caught by the poorly paid and often undocumented migrant workers, who cram them into the cages that will deliver them to a slaughterhouse where they will be disassembled on a factory line.

Very little, if anything, in this process honors or treats these chickens as gifts of God. Industrial methods of chicken production require that they fall within a *logos* or production system that stresses efficiency, uniformity and profitability. If we had the mind of Christ, however, and saw these creatures as having a role in God's new creation, we would think about what we can do to make sure that our relationships with chickens contributed to their nurture, health and even delight. Because Christ is the one through whom and for whom the whole world is created, chickens are part of his renewing ministry that leads all creatures into the fullness of life. Inspired and shaped by Christ's reconciling life, we must concern ourselves with the well-being of animals, working to make sure that they can live the life God intends for them. When we treat chickens the way God expects, which means that we devote ourselves to their care, shame disappears to make room for celebration.

EATING JESUS

Just as Jesus was known as the one who welcomed sinners and ate with them, the early Christian community that formed in faithfulness to him was known for its glad and generous eating. Speaking of the Christian followers formed at Pentecost, Luke records that "Day by day, as they spent much time together in the temple, they broke bread at home and ate their food with glad and generous hearts, praising God and having the goodwill of all the people" (Acts 2:46-47). We could say that Jesus had inspired them to eat in ways that bore witness to God's continuing presence.

Distinctly Christian forms of eating occur when Christ is present within us, enabling us to see, engage and taste the world in ways that are pleasing to him. As the apostle Paul put it, we should no longer consider others from a self-serving point of view. Instead, we should be so attuned to Jesus' way of being that we can say, "It is no longer I who live, but it is Christ who lives in me. And the life I now live in the flesh I live by faith in the Son of God, who loved me and gave himself for me" (Gal 2:20).

Intimacy with Christ, which is necessary for this kind of fidelity, can develop through the Eucharist, or Lord's Supper. Here Christians eat the body and drink the blood of Jesus so that he can nurture us into the life that bears witness to him. If we are what we eat, then eating Jesus should make us more like him.

Christians are not cannibals, of course. Luke's Gospel records that at the last Passover meal he ate with his disciples, Jesus gave thanks for a loaf of bread, broke it, gave it to them and said, "This is my body, which is given for you. Do this in remembrance in me." Similarly, he took a cup, saying, "This cup that is poured out for you is the new covenant in my blood" (Lk 22:19-20). At the Lord's table, Christians eat bread and drink the fruit of the vine so that Christ is drawn into the stomach and heart of our lives, energizing us for the life he makes possible. By remembering Jesus in our eating, we draw near enough to him that our thinking and feeling are transformed. Remembering is not the same as recalling a historical curiosity. It is, rather, inviting Jesus into our lives so that he can work within us the salvation that he incarnated.

John's Gospel describes this inner transformation in graphic terms. After describing himself as the "bread of life," Jesus said, "Very truly, I tell you, unless you eat the flesh of the Son of Man and drink his blood, you have no life in you. . . . for my flesh is true food and my blood is true drink. Those who eat my flesh and drink my blood abide in me, and I in them" (Jn 6:53-56). To eat and drink Jesus is to abide with him. It is to live because of him. When Christ abides in us—by our eating of him—our relationships with others are inspired and directed to take on his characteristics of attention, care, nurture, healing and reconciliation. These are the defining characteristics of Christ's life. The *Logos*, through whom the world is created and by which it is made fully alive, enters into us so that we can participate in genuine life.

For much of the Christian tradition, the Eucharist has been understood as a sacrificial meal. This is important because the high point of Jesus' ministry is his offering of himself to the point of death on a cross. The cross is not only an emblem of our violence and shame; it is also where God reveals definitively that true and abundant life consists in the complete and costly giving of oneself to another. The form of life that succeeds by grasping or hoarding or profiteering—abundantly on display in today's food production system and in fast-food eating patterns—is precisely the kind of life that Jesus came to correct through his own example. There is no resurrection life without the self-giving that the cross reveals.

The Eucharist, in other words, is not an occasional nibbling session in which Christians recall the violence done to their Lord. It is the table where we go to die ourselves. It is the regular time when we learn to put to death all the self-serving impulses that distort and degrade the world around us. Here we learn to live the baptism in which we die and are buried with Christ, so that we can also be raised with him into the newness of life that glorifies God rather than ourselves (see Rom 6:3-11). We die to sin so that we can be alive to God.

John's Gospel described this sacrificial movement using a

metaphor well known to farmers and gardeners: "Very truly, I tell you, unless a grain of wheat falls into the earth and dies, it remains just a single grain; but if it dies, it bears much fruit" (Jn 12:24). Jesus is not simply talking about seed. He is talking about the movement and fertility of life itself. God creates a world in which each creature can be a *giving* member to the whole. There is no life in isolation, fragmentation, alienation or withdrawal. This is why Jesus continued by saying, "Those who love their life lose it, and those who hate their life in this world will keep it for eternal life" (Jn 12:25). Witnessing to Christ's transforming presence and giving glory to God means offering ourselves to nurture others. At the Lord's Supper, Jesus nourishes us so that we can nourish the world around us.

It is tempting to confine eucharistic eating to a ritual realm. When this happens, the table around which Christians gather stays in a sanctuary. This is a serious error. The life and ministry of Jesus is not a pious idea. It is an economic revolution that has multiple practical effects, such that the tables in our kitchens and the dining tables in restaurants and cafeterias become places of eucharistic eating. Recall that the members of the early Christian community who gladly and generously ate together were also known to sell their possessions, give to those who had need and hold things in common. In a line that ought to astound us, Luke wrote, "There was not a needy person among them" (Acts 4:34). To eat in such a way that we abide in Christ and Christ abides in us means that we will give ourselves—our attention, our skills, our energy and our possessions—to others so that we all flourish. Eucharistic table manners result in sacrificial forms of living, in which meeting the needs of others is the defining concern.

We become agents of the "good news" that has been "proclaimed to every creature under heaven" when we become the kinds of eaters the Eucharist makes possible (Col 1:23). Eucharistic eating does not only transform the eating we do with people that happens at a particular table, as when we learn to become more attentive and hospitable to each other. It transforms the *entire* act of eating, which means it changes the way we go about growing, harvesting, processing, distributing, preparing and then sharing the food we daily eat.

EUCHARISTIC EATING IN ACTION

What would self-offering look like if we tried to realize it in today's industrial food system? To answer this question, we need to make an important distinction between self-offering and self-imposition. Out of a well-meaning desire to do good or simply get by, we may too easily impose a plan on others that we think will be to our mutual benefit. So a farmer may, for instance, look at a field and determine that he or she should grow a lot of potatoes. Growing a lot of potatoes is good, because then there is more food to feed the world. To maximize yield, the farmer will also use synthetic fertilizers and a regular cocktail of poisons to deal with potato plant pests. This scenario follows the *logos* of industrial potato production.

What is missing in this *logos* is the desire first and always to *attend* to the land. In an industrial system, land is simply viewed as a resource to satisfy aims that may or may not be good for the land itself. Here land is reduced to whatever human ambition imposes upon it. Little thought is given to how the imposition may result in considerable harm to the soil, water, plants, animals and humans that nourish themselves in this toxic site. Attending to the land means keeping a variety of questions in mind: how much soil is being eroded or degraded with this agricultural technique? What is the quality of the groundwater in the area owing to the steady stream of fertilizers and herbicides? Are the microorganisms in the soil healthy and thriving, and so daily contributing to the fertility of the soil? What is the nutrient quality of the potato that is grown in industrial conditions? Are the workers in the fields safe and fairly treated and compensated? Answering these questions requires clear and detailed vision. You have to get close and stay there to determine what is really going on.

During the civil rights movement, it became apparent that genuine reconciliation between people would not be possible unless whites and blacks physically *relocated* so as to be in close and sustained proximity to each other. People need to dwell in ways that allow them to see each other's pains and joys, limits and potential. Although legal integration of school districts is possible through the efforts of people who may not deeply know or care about each other, the reconciliation that defines a beloved community is not possible from a distance or via a bureaucratic *logos*. Community presupposes people who are ready to offer themselves to each other so that personal desire is overtaken by a desire for the other. Following the apostle Paul's formulation, community means holding the needs, desires and joys of others such that my own needs, desires and enjoyments make no sense apart from the life we live *together*. Only then can people become the sort of community that functions like an organic body—no member or part alone, but all working together to be a healthy whole.

Reconciliation with the land requires a similar kind of relocation. For much of human history, we have not really attended to or known the land that nourishes us. In our hubris and neglect we have thus exhausted, degraded and destroyed much of it. In our ambition we have ruined where we are and then moved on to "virgin territory" or "greener pastures." We have not settled our land in ways that indicate our respect and care for other creatures. Nor have we given due consideration to the limits and potential latent within every habitat. The history of American settlement witnesses to a *logos* of exploitation in which the machinery of bulldozers, guns, dynamite, dams and poison have imposed our will on the world.

Put in more theological terms, we have failed to appreciate that creation forms a vast and indescribably complex and organic whole. Humanity is only one member within this creation. It does not all exist for our exclusive benefit. As God reminded Job, the earth is full of creatures that are of no use to us but are of intimate concern to God: "Who provides for the raven its prey, when its young ones cry to God, and wander about for lack of food?" (Job 38:41). It contains creatures like the mighty Leviathan, which can kill us but is a particular delight to God: "I will not keep silence concerning its limbs, or its mighty strength, or its splendid frame" (Job 41:12).

Creation exists for our health and nurture, but it is not made for our exclusive enjoyment. When we become attentive, we quickly learn that there is much within it that can harm or even kill us. Not everything that looks good is edible. We have to be careful and knowledgeable. We also have to be respectful. We have to learn that sometimes it is best to let creatures and their places alone. Above all, we need to make ourselves students of the places where we live, which will instruct us in the ways of faithful living. That is where self-offering begins.

To gain a sense for what is practically involved, we can turn to The Land Institute in Salina, Kansas. Begun over thirty years ago by plant geneticist Wes Jackson, The Land Institute is working to develop an agriculture that nourishes rather than depletes the land. Its mission statement reads: "When people, land, and community are as one, all three members prosper; when they relate not as members but as competing interests, all three are exploited. By consulting Nature as the source and measure of that membership, The Land Institute seeks to develop an agriculture that will save soil from being lost or poisoned while promoting a community life at once prosperous and enduring."

To get to the heart of Jackson's thinking, we have to appreciate the complexity of the responsibilities that accompany our membership in the world. He argues that with the birth of agriculture ten thousand years ago, humanity began its assault on the land, thus putting all future memberships in peril. Readers of Scripture are inclined to see the invention of the plow as a sign of peace and prosperity, and perhaps even to make an appeal to the prophetic declaration that in the peaceable days to come, nations will "beat their swords into plowshares, and their spears into pruning hooks" (Is 2:4). The truth of history, however, is that till agriculture has decimated and compromised much of the earth's soil. Turning the soil upside down has exposed it to wind and water erosion. Tearing apart its root structures has compromised the soil's ability to hold moisture and maintain a rich microbial life.

This is why Jackson and his team of scientists at The Land Institute are developing a perennial, polyculture form of agriculture. If we are to have an agriculture that does not exploit the land, it needs to grow perennial plants, which have deep root structures that hold soil and water together. We need to move away from vast fields of monoculture in which commodities like corn, wheat and soy are replanted year after year. A monoculture system depends on the plow and the heavy use of synthetic, fossil-fuel-derived fertilizers and toxic herbicides. Instead, we must move toward fields that grow multiple kinds of plants together, such as nitrogen-fixing legumes with nitrogen-needing grains. Such combinations provide pest protection and nutrient enhancement. The key to it all, says Jackson, is learning how creation grows without poisons and artificial fertilizers. We must make nature "the source and measure" of our membership with the land, as The Land Institute's mission statement reads.

Making natural systems agriculture a reality will require a massive shift in government policy. For that to happen, food consumers need to demand from their elected officials policies that put the health of land and people above the massive profits by a handful of agricultural companies. Advocates like Jackson, Wendell Berry, Herman Daly and Fred Kirschenmann have been arguing that we need to scrap today's Farm Bill, which keeps our fields in land-destroying monoculture. We need to replace it with a Fifty-Year Farm Bill that promotes an agriculture that runs on sunshine (rather than fossil fuel), builds soil fertility, preserves clean water, eliminates massive animal confinement operations and protects plant and animal diversity. We need to understand that a farm bill is really a food bill, and thus also an energy bill and a health bill. When we recognize how the wars of our world constantly center on the desire for the resources drawn from land and water, it is not a stretch to say that our farm bill is also always a defense bill.

The Land Institute teaches that whatever farming we develop in the future must fit the ecosystem in which it occurs. That means that in Kansas, we must learn to farm like the prairie. We must become students of prairie ways of sustaining plant diversity and plant growth, ways that over the centuries have built fertility rather than diminished it. When we do this, we demonstrate that we have relocated our vision and desire so that our agricultural practices develop in response to the needs and potential of the land and are not an imposition upon it. As *members* of the land, rather than bandits of it, we learn the skills and disciplines that promote mutual flourishing. By taking the time to understand where we are and how best to live gently and gratefully there, we participate in God's gardening ways, which give and ennoble life. We discover the world to be beautiful, fertile, dangerous, mysterious, fragrant and delectable. And so we come to share in God's Sabbath joy.

SAYING GRACE

When I was growing up, my family would pray this German blessing before each meal: *Segne, Vater, diese Speise, uns zur Kraft und dir zum Preise.* It can be roughly translated as, "Bless, dear Father, these thy gifts, given for our strength and for your praise."

It may be tempting to dismiss our ritual action as the pious relic of a bygone era. But what if saying grace at mealtimes is an essential expression of our creaturely dependence, and therefore also a declaration of our responsibilities to God, each other and the land? Might it not be an indispensable reminder to receive land and life as precious gifts to be nurtured, shared and celebrated?

To say grace is to offer thanksgiving to God for the food we are about to eat. Thanksgiving is a complex act. It presupposes that we know what we are being thankful for. It assumes that we find what we are about to eat of value and thus worthy of thanks. It entails the kind of humility in which people readily bow their heads before raising their forks. None of this can be taken for granted in our industrial, fast-food world.

It is becoming common knowledge that much of the food on our plates travels hundreds or even thousands of miles to get there. The transcontinental head of lettuce grown in California but eaten in Boston or New York not only travels through the clouds of our atmosphere. It also makes its way through a vast cloud of consumer ignorance, in which eaters have no idea where the lettuce came from, how the land it grew on was farmed, what toxic inputs were used and how the farmworkers were treated. The lettuce simply arrives, shorn of its ecological and cultural contexts. If one were to express gratitude for it, what exactly would one be saying thank you for?

When food registers primarily as a product or commodity, the focus of our thinking goes straight to the sticker price. The scope of our concern might include taste and nutritional content, but because we are so ignorant about food's agricultural and economic contexts, we don't really have much patience or appreciation for its gracious life. What I mean by food's grace is an experience known to every farmer and gardener: food is an inexhaustible mystery. Life is a fragile and vulnerable gift we hardly understand, much less control. Although we prepare the ground, plant the seed and then nurture the plant, a good harvest and a delicious meal depend on so many gifts from God that we can hardly enumerate them. Soil decomposition, photosynthesis, hydrological cycles, plant and animal health, pollination, pollinators and animal reproduction: it is easy to take these gifts for granted. It is dangerous, too, if we begin to think that nothing we do puts these gifts in jeopardy.

When we sit down at the table and fill our plates, how many of us take the time to carefully consider the wonder and the fragility of what is there? The Shakers had the practice of observing a time of silence before eating. This is important for us, too, so that we can calm our minds, tame our egos and then mindfully receive the gracious gift of food. Are we not startled by the fact that God created a world that tastes so good? Are we not perpetually amazed that a grain of wheat can be transformed into the many kinds of breads and cakes and cookies that make our life a joy? Saying grace matters because it opens our imaginations (and our stomachs) to the marvelous creation that makes our eating and fellowship possible and a potential delight. Since our mouths enable us to eat *and* kiss, should we not prepare and devote our hearts for eating much like we prepare and devote our hearts for kissing?

Every bite of food is an introduction to God's particular joy in a creature's being. Being trained at the eucharistic table means learning to savor each morsel as a delectable manifestation of God's love. Appreciation of this sort takes time and preparation to develop. The taste that genuinely savors the world as God's own simply cannot be rushed. We need the daily reminder of saying grace before every meal.

Because saying grace is an act of faithfulness before God, it is also a political and economic act. It has to be. We cannot express gratitude to God for the gifts of food if, in our production and consumption practices, we are degrading those gifts. The grateful speech that remembers and names the items on our plate, and that honors the biophysical, farming and cooking processes that made them possible, must not at the same time reflect our destruction of the world. We remember God and creation at mealtimes so that we can become participants in the *re*membering of the creation that is too often being *dis*-membered by us.

When we appreciate how saying grace strengthens the memberships of creation, we also see that saying grace is a reconciling act. Being reconciled with each other means being in the presence of each other without shame. It presupposes that we have committed to make our lives into an offering of time, energy and skill that serves the need and the potential of others. When we say grace in an authentic way, our presence in the world becomes good news. The creatures we eat and those we eat with can be assured that our desire abides in God's desire that all creatures taste the heavenly delight that daily creates and sustains the world.

6

Bread for the
Whole Body of Christ

FRED BAHNSON

For many are the trees of God that grow
In Paradise, and various, yet unknown
To us, in such abundance lies our choice.

JOHN MILTON, *PARADISE LOST*, BOOK IX

During the flight into Fort Myers, Florida, I looked down on a vast, oil-driven network of fast-food chains, malls and suburbs, little fiefdoms of fancy destined for ruin in the sunshine-powered future. Standing an hour later at the Global Farm sponsored by the Educational Concerns for Hunger Organization (ECHO), I felt that the contrast couldn't have been more stark. It was like stepping into the Nigerian village

I lived in as a missionary kid, albeit one with lots of white people. Instead of running on oil, this place derived most of its energy from contemporary sunlight. Aside from a golfcart here and there, everyone walked or rode bikes.

Now it's eight o'clock in the morning and I am standing at the base of perhaps the only mountain in southwest Florida. Actually, it's more of a hill. According to the plaque in front of me, this fifty-foot-high bulldozer-built mound is called the Tropical Highlands. The plaque's description reads: "steep land subject to severe eroding." Before-and-after photographs of a Honduran hillside show a denuded slope next to the same slope years later, this time lush and verdant. Like the hillside in front of me.

Joel Wildasin is the intern in charge of this part of ECHO's Global Farm. Uphill on the right he points to several terraces, a good method to slow erosion, but on the hill's left side is a better system. It's called SALT: Sloping Agricultural Land Technology, an intercropping pattern that alternates perennial hedgerows with annual cash crops. According to the folks here at ECHO, the SALT system outperforms terraces when growing crops on steep tropical hillsides. I carefully study the left-hand slope. At first the overall effect is one of contained chaos; there are just too many different kinds of plants here to make sense of. Then I begin to see. There are three hedgerows roughly seventy-five-feet long and spaced at intervals of twelve feet, each hugging the slope's contour. Within the hedgerows are at least four or five species of shrubs and trees. As perennial polycultures, the hedgerows serve many purposes. They keep soil and water on the slope. They attract insect-eating birds. Some of the hedgerow plants fix nitrogen. Others, like fish poison bean, tephrosia and neem, have insecticidal uses. With these hedgerows, you're growing both your own fertilizer and your own insecticides, with cash crops in between. Joel points out the demonstration plots of strawberries nestled comfortably among the hedgerows on the twenty-degree slope. This SALT plot is a carefully designed system that mimics a natural ecosystem's polyculture, in which each interlinking part supports and enhances its neighbor.

It is such agricultural clearheadedness that I have come to witness and that has gained ECHO the respect of development organizations around the world. Here nature is not a series of problems that stand in the way of human agriculture, but a model—a standard—on which to base that agriculture. As I look at the hillside before me, I also muse that places like this will become tiny arks to which people will turn when the waters of trouble—climate change, fossil-fuel depletion and resulting food shortages—start to rise. For that reason, ECHO's Global Farm is much more than just a place to teach food-growing techniques for the tropics. It is a model for how humans can not only survive coming catastrophes but flourish.

And yet I find among the people here no self-righteous prophets, no smug doomsayers. Joel and the others at ECHO are hopeful because they know the bounty the land can produce, even in places as desolate as Keefa, Mauritania, where ECHO's CEO Stan Doerr and his wife, Beth, helped plant two hundred tire gardens in what was once a desert. "Redemption doesn't just start after we die," said ECHO's seed-bank manager Tim Motis; "We can begin to experience life in all its abundance right here on earth."

Abundance is a word I heard often on the lips of ECHO workers. They aren't just trying to end hunger; they want to help people tap into creation's fecundity, an abundance in nature that was there all along, waiting to be discovered and shared.

ECHO's witness is a fitting capstone to our story of God's call to reconciliation with the land, because it challenges the misconstrued idea that the agrarian concerns we've described are only important for North Americans. The folks here at ECHO remind us that shalom on the land begins when we focus our energy on those who have been excluded from the table, when we share our knowledge and thus offer them the seat of honor.

THE HUNGER SEASON

When BBC America aired its story on the global food crisis last year, it wasn't the Food and Agriculture Organization or the World Food Program they profiled as a model. It was ECHO. "And now," the commentator said, "here's a group that's actually doing something about it [the food crisis]."

ECHO's fifty-acre campus lies just north of the Caloosahatchee River. An interdenominational Christian organization, ECHO was founded in 1981 and now serves as a tropical agricultural training center for development workers in 180 countries. With the global food crisis expected to worsen, ECHO is increasingly looked to as an organization with answers. Their mission is "to network with community leaders in developing countries to seek hunger solutions for families growing food under difficult conditions." That last part about "difficult conditions" is where they really shine. The staff here have become experts at growing crops in the harsh environments—deserts, eroded hillsides and slum rooftops—in which the very poor often live. They describe their organization as "an extension agent to the world," especially to developing countries that don't have resources like land-grant universities and extension agents. Considering that 75 percent of the world's poor live in rural areas with limited communication access, that's a big gap for an organization based in southwest Florida to fill. Yet it struck me that with forty-three staff—eleven of whom are scientists—and 450 volunteers, ECHO essentially *is* a land-grant university, albeit one that doesn't depend on federal money.

In addition to research, ECHO provides free consulting for development workers. If you're stumped with an irrigation problem in Zambia and need some advice, you can email an ECHO staff member, who will usually respond within a day or two. They post free documents on their website, which averages nine hundred downloads a day. Also, any organization or individual working to help the exceptionally poor in a developing country can write to ECHO and request trial packets of seeds from their extensive tropical seed bank. If the crop does well, they can save their seed and are then expected to report back on the plant's performance.

The most impressive place on ECHO's fifty-acre campus

is the Global Farm. On twelve acres of what was originally beach sand, ECHO's staff have mimicked six thriving tropical ecosystems, each demonstrating a host of sustainable agriculture practices appropriate to that region. I was unprepared for just how edenic, how ecologically exuberant this place would be. Browsing my way through these ecosystems, where nearly every one of the 580 varieties of vegetables, trees and shrubs are edible, I experienced a feeling of limitless bounty. I now fully understood the phrase *edible landscape*. Over the course of my three-day visit, I ate my way across twelve acres and six ecosystems; each zone was a new restaurant. In the various orchards I gobbled yellow loquats, ruby red grapefruit, blood oranges and numerous *calamunda*, a year-round citrus fruit the size of a golf ball. I munched cranberry hibiscus leaves in the Semi-Arid Tropics, moringa leaves in the Hot Humid Lowlands and Tropical Monsoon and strawberries and mulberries in the Tropical Highlands. In the Urban Rooftop Garden I nibbled sugar snap peas, carrots and garlic chives that had been growing in an old tire for the past thirteen years. In the Rainforest—an acre-sized zone of raised garden beds, palm trees, drainage moats and overhead sprinkler systems— I shimmied up a palm tree and cut down three big coconuts: one to take back to my four-year-old son, one to give to Andrew (the ECHO intern who loaned me his machete for the purpose) and one for me. I chopped mine open and slurped down the milk in one gulp. I became Adam in all his prelapsarian glory, sating himself with creation's delights.

I spent a good chunk of time in the Hot Humid Lowlands,

a flat expanse of raised beds, sugar cane and rice paddies interplanted with palms and papaya. Two of the most important plants that grow in this part of the Global Farm are edible perennials: chaya, a shrub, and moringa, a tree. Each pack a big nutritional load, and each grows well in poor tropical soils.

Chaya is sometimes called "tree spinach"; its palm-sized leaves remind me of the okra plant. Chaya contains cyanide, not a winning ingredient in anyone's salad, but one that works to your advantage. The cyanide provides a deterrent for goats or other animals who might be wandering around your yard. By boiling the leaves for ten minutes you can remove the toxin, making chaya a safe and nutritious green high in both protein and vitamin C.

With no access to a cookstove I couldn't sample the chaya, but the leaves on the moringa tree are edible in raw form. *Moringa oleifera,* also known as "the miracle tree," is native to India (known there as "drumstick") and grows naturally in many tropical areas around the world. Only recently, after ECHO began promoting it heavily, have researchers and development workers begun to realize its huge potential to stave off malnutrition. Most moringa programs promote its use in home gardens and health clinics in severely impoverished countries. Gram for gram, moringa contains twice the protein of yogurt, four times the vitamin A of carrots, and seven times the vitamin C of oranges. I pick a leaf and chew it. The taste is peppery and bright, like arugula. Though money may not grow on trees, it appears that multivitamins do.

For the poor in tropical regions, there comes a time each

year toward the end of the dry season when food is scarce, a time when eating next year's seed becomes a tempting thought: the hunger season. During this difficult time, which descends like an unwanted guest, hardy plants like chaya and moringa quickly take on a special significance. Depending on when the rains come, the hunger season is measured in weeks or months. Sometimes, during drought or war or times of political corruption, the hunger season is measured in years. Or lifetimes.

HUNGER: A PRIMER

Before coming to ECHO, I had the vague and mistaken notion that world hunger was simply about a lack of food. After all, wasn't that the aim of the Green Revolution: to increase yields so that there would be more food all around?

In his groundbreaking 1981 book *Poverty and Famines*, Nobel laureate Amartya Sen demonstrated that starvation resulted not from a lack of food but from its unfair distribution. "Starvation is the characteristic of some people not *having* enough food to eat," he wrote, "not the characteristic of there *being* not enough food to eat." Given that assessment, I wondered, why does ECHO focus on teaching small-scale farming skills that boost production? Why not focus their efforts on changing bad policies?

"I didn't want to become 'God's Angry Young Man,'" said Martin Price, ECHO's founder. Martin is a small, unassuming man in his sixties, whose quiet demeanor seems more fitted to the staid life of the biochem lab than to directing a thriving nonprofit organization. Since turning over the reins in 2006 to ECHO's current CEO, Stan Doerr, Martin now volunteers at ECHO, refining the rooftop gardening techniques he has worked on for almost half of his adult life.

Early on, Martin decided that he wanted to come out with solutions. He agreed with Amartya Sen's assessment that anybody with money can get food. "You can have an oil kingdom in the desert where nothing grows, and you can purchase all the food you want," Martin said, "but if you're poor, you need either a source of income or you need to grow that food yourself."

The only time it doesn't make sense to focus on food production is in totally imploded societies: refugee situations, for instance, or civil war, in which people have no control over their lives. But for the most part, the politics of a country aren't connecting with impoverished farmers. "You can talk about corrupt governance in Zimbabwe," said Stan, an avuncular, bearded man in his fifties, "but if people can maximize productivity on their piece of land, they will have more say in their future." By helping the small farmer, Stan and Martin and others at ECHO believe, you increase food security for the whole country. You reduce urbanization because people no longer need to leave their farm for the city. If a country is not stable politically, then land tenure is a problem for small farmers. If the country *is* stable politically but nobody knows how to grow food, that's unsustainable, too. Take the antipodes of Sudan and the United States. In Sudan many people want to farm, but until recently they could not for fear of political violence. In the United States, 99 percent of the population not only don't *want* to farm but don't know how.

"The big picture in fighting hunger is that somebody needs to come along and tackle the really tough problem of making marginal land more productive in a sustainable way," Martin told me. "It's not as glamorous as, say, treating two hundred kids for worms or starting a microlending program. But it's the bottom-line solution to poverty."

To that end, ECHO focuses on underexploited food plants. Of all the food eaten in the world, 95 percent of it comes from only thirty species. "And yet God has created many, many kinds of food plants," Martin said. Maybe corn isn't the best thing for your region; maybe the grain amaranth is better. Or in semi-arid Brazil, the egusi melon, with seeds containing 50 percent oil and 30 percent protein, might be a better choice.

Martin is careful to point out that ECHO isn't promoting an ideology or program. Although ECHO practices what I would consider regenerative agriculture, they still occasionally use fertilizers and pesticides, albeit in limited amounts. They simply want to present options, believing that the farmers themselves should be given all the available knowledge and then decide what works best for them. There's a big difference between pouring a bottle-cap of fertilizer in the bottom of a hole you've dug for your corn, Martin reminded me, and spraying a whole field with it.

Sitting in Stan's office on the first day of my visit, I asked him how ECHO confronts agriculture's role in global warming. "I look forward to global warming," Stan said with a wink. "It's too cold here in southwest Florida." Joking aside, Stan told me that ECHO works primarily with techniques that make both good economic sense and good environmental sense: for example, using compost, which both increases soil fertility and sequesters carbon in the soil, or biodigesters, contraptions that capture methane from animal manure. These can reduce or eliminate the need for firewood. Instead of cutting down trees, you take your manure, capture the methane and cook with it. The carbon dioxide released when you cook is absorbed by the trees that you didn't have to cut down, and later that manure can be applied to your soil.

Dedication to improving the lives of the poor was what especially impressed me about the staff at ECHO. It is their vocation. "If you want to find God, then go to the poor," Stan said, "because that's where God is. I think that's why Jesus had compassion on them, because they were harassed on every side. When you're downtrodden as the poor often are, you just think this is the way it's going to be forever. Like the Dalits in India—you think you deserve what you're getting. And that's just not the case. God didn't intend for children to go hungry."

Jesus' parable of the sheep and the goats in Matthew's Gospel has always reminded Stan of his responsibility to the poor. The parable tells of Jesus' return, when he will gather all the nations before him and separate people one from another, "as a shepherd separates the sheep from the goats" (Mt 25:32). The sheep will be those who fed their neighbor, who was really Jesus in disguise, and they will be rewarded. The goats are those who saw the hungry and gave them no food, and because of their hardheartedness, they were sent packing. Stan wants to be counted among the sheep.

The phone rings. It's one of the interns from the farm calling. Stan picks up, listens a minute, then says, "Just make certain you get the testicles down low enough so that you're not squashing them. You want to get some of those seminal tubules."

He hangs up and says, "Castrating goats."

SOLUTIONS: ANOTHER GREEN REVOLUTION OR REGENERATIVE AGRICULTURE?

During one stroll in the Hot Humid Lowlands, I noticed several rice paddies that Stan would later describe as demonstration plots for a new method of growing rice. Back in the 1970s, a priest in Madagascar discovered what is now called SRI—System of Rice Intensification—which, despite its big name, is actually very simple. Instead of planting a cluster of seedlings in each hole in a flooded field, you plant one seedling per hole in a nonflooded field. In a cluster, all those seedlings compete with each other. But if you plant one seedling, that plant will produce tillers, which are side shoots that each carry a seed head. Guess what? Those tillers are no longer competing with each other; they're working together off the same root system. "Rice grows in a flooded field not because it *has to* but because it *can*," Stan said. Take away the water, and you've suddenly allowed more oxygen to reach those roots. By using the SRI technique, you've increased yield 100 to 150 percent, and you've used one-tenth the seed.

ECHO is a repository of such ideas that, for the most part, Stan and his coworkers have learned from small farmers, development workers and other agricultural researchers. The SRI's high yields are not due to increased fertilizer or hybrid seeds, as was the case with the Green Revolution. They are the result of discovering how nature creates abundance— in this case, allowing each plant the space to grow without competition—and mimicking it. Such horticultural plenitude doesn't just happen, of course. It takes patience and skill, as well as an awareness of human temptation to reach beyond our limits. We're slow to learn that the tree of knowledge contains both good and evil.

It was through an effort to bypass nature and create abundance from scratch that the first Green Revolution began. Coined by William Gaud, director of the U.S. Agency for International Development, in 1968, the phrase *Green Revolution* has come to signify the major shift toward industrial agriculture that began in the Yaqui Valley in Mexico during World War II and culminated in India and other parts of Asia in the 1960s and 1970s. Funded by the Rockefeller and Ford Foundations, the Green Revolution was perhaps the largest project aimed at ending global hunger the world has ever seen. It was also humanity's biggest attempt thus far to create the illusion of abundance through chemistry.

To create this biological sleight of hand, the Green Revolution's magicians, notably plant breeder Norman Borlaug, developed new varieties of wheat and rice. These super-plants produced abundantly, but the monocultures in which they were grown required massive amounts of irrigation, fertilizers and pesticides. Instead of a polyculture of crops, you had one crop. Soil *biology* was replaced with soil *chemistry*. As its promoters and detractors alike claim, the Green Revolution boosted short-term yields and fed millions of people. But every revolution must eventually take stock of its successes and failures, and the ecological bills on the Green Revolution's account are now coming due. The world is in the red: dead zones in our oceans, poisoned groundwater, salinized soils. Punjab, the breadbasket of India and former crown jewel of the Green Revolution, is now a wasteland. It's true that Borlaug's "miracle seeds," under the right circumstances, could provide "an abundance that was almost certain," Raj Patel wrote in *Stuffed and Starved: The Hidden Battle for the World Food System*. "The problem lay in the fact that the circumstances were almost never right." The new seeds required excessive irrigation, which caused water tables to drop over a foot a year; such irrigation also caused salts to build in the soils, turning them lifeless; the turn toward monoculture eradicated indigenous biodiversity; and the repeated use of petrochemicals led to not only poor soil health, but poisoned wells and high cancer rates. Patel summarized the Green Revolution as "basically the use of industrial technology to avoid dealing with tough social questions. It removed the sting from land reform and represents the triumph of technological thinking versus more sustainable ways of addressing the hunger crisis."

Given the grim results of the Green Revolution, it is disturbing to hear that the Gates Foundation is trying to mount the "next Green Revolution" in Africa. Through partner organizations like the Alliance for a Green Revolution in Africa, African Agricultural Technology Foundation and the Monsanto Corporation, Gates aims to improve African agriculture in the neediest countries by a combination of free-market fixes and genetically modified, drought-tolerant maize.

Gates would do well to heed the 2008 report from the International Assessment of Agricultural Knowledge, Science, and Technology for Development (IAASTD) mentioned in chapter two. A collaboration of over four hundred scientists and development specialists, IAASTD found that industrial agricultural practices, including genetically modified crops, do not address the complex challenges of local agriculture and often produce environmental harm. The Green Revolution's proponents argue that the only way we'll be able to feed the world is through genetically modified crops, chemical pesticides and fertilizers. Organic farmers have long known that myth to be false, but the IAASTD report has finally debunked it with incontrovertible evidence. The answer they propose is agroecology, what I referred to in chapter four as regenerative agriculture.

Which is exactly the kind of work that, without much fanfare or recognition, ECHO has been quietly doing for the past thirty years.

THE NEW AGRICULTURAL FRONTIER?

On my last day at ECHO, I paid a visit to the Urban Rooftop Garden to see firsthand what has become a major focus of ECHO's work around the world. This demonstration area mimics the flat concrete rooftops and tin shacks you might find in the slums of Kibera, Mexico City or, before the earthquake, Port au Prince. Martin Price looks at the roofs above peoples' heads as huge untapped "fields" on which food can be grown. Rooftop gardening was, in fact, part of Martin's original vision for ECHO. On a trip to Port au Prince in the early 1980s, Martin looked out over acres of flat concrete roofs. An urban rooftop is only a staircase away from a market. Here, he realized, was agriculture's final frontier.

On top of the concrete pad in front of me were more than fifty demonstration garden beds made out of various recycled items: old tires, carpet, bamboo. The car tires, filled with compost and sitting on top of concrete blocks, were placed at waist-level for easy access and contained everything from eggplant to strawberries. To my left a plastic kids' pool, filled to the brim with lightweight mulch and compost, grew a healthy crop of sweet peppers.

I was greeted by Andrew Kroeze, a soft-spoken intern who maintains the garden. He explained that limiting factor on such roofs is weight; too much imported topsoil will cause a roof to leak or even collapse. Other growing mediums are needed—things easily found in poor countries, such as soda cans, which serve as the "soil" for a bed of habanero peppers. The beds are built like this: an impermeable layer of plastic is laid on the concrete. On top of that goes an old carpet. A border of bricks, laid in a rectangle, delineates the size of the bed. Inside the bricks, a layer of soda cans is added to provide volume. Eight-week-old peppers are then transplanted into the soda-can "soil." As the plants grow, their roots are protected from the desiccating effects of wind and sun by the soda cans, which also prop up the plants. Every day or two a five-gallon bucket with a hole poked in the lid is upturned on a small, exposed section of carpet, watering the entire bed with compost tea. The carpet wicks the tea down the length of the bed, feeding each pepper plant as much as it needs.

I walked past other garden beds that use materials as diverse as bamboo, pea gravel and even old tennis shoes. Martin's criteria are that the beds must be low weight and inexpensive, give satisfactory production with minimal inputs, contain no moving parts and be made from local and preferably recycled materials: in other words, *trash*.

The backbone of the Urban Rooftop Garden's fertility program is a flock of caged chickens. These birds eat refuse from the garden as well as store-bought grain. They provide not only eggs and meat but also the raw materials for compost tea, which will feed the plants. The chicken poop goes into a fifty-gallon drum. "But you've got to let it soak for at least three weeks before you water plants with it," Andrew warned.

Martin's dream is to one day go to Port au Prince or Mumbai and see acres and acres of rooftop gardens. But that would be only the beginning. "Even if there were no more hunger, I'd still be doing what I'm doing," he told me. "I'd like to see small rural farms become so productive that people leave the slums and return to the countryside. Eliminating hunger and malnutrition is just the first step. There is just so much more to life than not being hungry."

FROM THE HUNGER SEASON
TO THE ABUNDANT TABLE

The abundance that God grants in the seed and soil cannot be forced. It can only be coaxed. Any solutions to hunger, any method of procuring our daily sustenance, must henceforth begin by recognizing our ecological limits.

All of the standard hunger narratives imply a lacuna, an empty bracket in the full sentence of a human life. Most of us accept perpetual hunger for some as a sad but unavoidable reality. But when we, the amply fed, accept the myth that the hunger season will never end for *those* Haitians, *those* Sudanese, *that* homeless guy in the stoplight meridian, we starve our imaginations. We become inwardly stunted human beings, malnourished souls. Maybe the very word *hunger* has lost its linguistic currency. We need new words, new stories, because the old ones raise too many hackles, induce too much crippling guilt and distract us from the important work ahead.

What we need are stories about how people are not only avoiding hunger but are living *well*. Such stories are myriad. Physically joining our own lives to such stories can be a hedge against our innate capacity for greed. It can help us see the abundant way of living to which Jesus calls us. I think of the perennial hedgerows on that hillside, how they work in tandem to create a beautiful and teeming symmetry, and of Stan's rice tillers, the ones that are no longer competing with each other but instead share the same root system, how they grow to produce a hundredfold.

The word *hunger* is a negation; it represents a deviation from the norm.

And what is the norm? It is the great messianic feast all yearn to see, and of which we are offered a foretaste even now. It is all of us seated at God's table. It is *shared abundance*.

Epilogue

. . . So We Can Eat from the Tree of Life

Then the angel showed me the river of the water of life, bright as crystal,
flowing from the throne of God and of the Lamb through the middle
of the street of the city. On either side of the river, is the tree of life
with its twelve kinds of fruit, producing its fruit each month;
and the leaves of the tree are for the healing of the nations.

REVELATION 22:1-2

What does the "tree of life" look like? What will its twelve kinds of fruit taste like? Will it have pears, firm and juicy, or persimmons, whose orange pulp is soft and sweet? Or will the tree of life be more like the multipurpose moringa tree, whose leaves, roots and seeds are useful to human and animal alike? And what is this tree growing in? Would that we could sink our hands into and smell the soil out of which this tree grows. It must be the richest and liveliest soil the world has ever known. Surely this tree's colors are the most beautiful and welcoming people have ever seen. Why else would people from all the nations want to come?

The human story in Scripture began in a garden with fruit and seed-bearing trees that were both beautiful and delicious (see Gen 1:29-31). Its soil was fertile beyond imagining, bringing forth "living creatures of every kind" (Gen 1:24). In the middle of the Garden of Eden, surrounded by trees that were "pleasant to the sight and good for food," stood the tree of life (Gen 2:9). We have hardly known this tree, since in fits of hubris we have banished ourselves from its fruit and shade.

The garden was also the source of the river that divided into four branches (Pishon, Gihon, Tigris and Euphrates) that watered the lands of the known world. Living in an arid climate, the writers of Scripture knew well how important water is. Fertile land, bountiful seeds, beautiful trees, living creatures of every kind: none of these can survive without the cool, fresh, life-giving water that rivers provide.

But the history of humanity is a history of deforestation and water waste. Although it may be hard to imagine this now, well over half of North America and most of Europe, Brazil, Asia and Indonesia were once covered in forests. We need these forests; besides being the lungs of our planet, they are home to countless species of plants and animals.

It seems that we are determined to eliminate the trees. We are systematically cutting them down to make room for agriculture, mines and roads, and to feed our want of wood, paper and fiber. In destroying the forests we also undermine the climate, food and energy flows that make our earth a viable home.

Meanwhile, glaciers (summer's water "banks") are receding, underground aquifers are being depleted at an unsustainable rate and many of the world's major rivers (the Colorado, Nile, Ganges and Yellow) periodically run dry before they reach their ocean destinations. Nearly 60 percent of major rivers are now dammed or fragmented in some significant way, either for power generation or to create reservoirs for agricultural and recreational purposes. This compromises the forests, fields and wetlands that depend on water's flow.

How much of human history is opposed to life? How much of civilization is premised on creation's destruction? To take part in God's reconciliation of the world is not to pine after some lost Eden. It is to live in anticipation of the New Jerusalem, the heavenly city come down to earth.

At the end of Scripture, the place where the eternal Gardener's desire is fulfilled, we find again the river and the tree. But something remarkable has happened: "the throne of God and the Lamb will be in it . . . they will see his face, and his name will be on their foreheads" (Rev 22:3-4). In Genesis, God was present and was known to walk in the garden (see Gen 3:8). This is why Adam and Eve hid behind a tree, hoping they could escape God's presence and God's questioning.

But in the end, there is no hiding from God behind trees. There can't be, because the tree of life has the throne of God and the Lamb *in it*, suffusing the tree with God's nurturing, creating and delighting presence from every angle. God is so close that nothing escapes his life-giving light. God is so close that the sun and moon are no longer necessary (see Rev 22:5).

In this new garden, there is no night. The presence of God is so intense that our vision is now completely enfolded within his seeing, sustaining embrace of the world. The divine breath that lifts us up from the soil and animates us from within is now revealed to us as the song and rhythm within our life. It enables us to finally receive and welcome the whole world as one unfathomable melody of love.

Here, at the end of days, when the Lamb who was slaughtered reconciles all things to himself, we are told that *heaven descends to earth*. God comes down from heaven so that he can make his home *with us*, and God brings heaven along. Here we encounter the good news that creation is not going to burn or be "left behind" while a few anemic souls fly away to some distant heaven. No, the once-distant heaven now takes root in earthly soil. "The home of God is among mortals" (Rev 21:3).

You might say that the way God redeems the world is to make the world more fully *it*self, just as the way God redeems us makes us more fully *ourselves*. That's what our belief in the resurrection of the body means. And the world around us will become part of that resurrected glory.

In the new heaven and new earth, we discover that we have never been alone. We have only ever been nurtured and loved. Although we have done everything we can to separate ourselves from other people, from creatures large and small, from the land and its waters and from God, God has never left us. God the Gardener comes every day, bucket and hoe in hand, to water and weed the soil of our lives. Through God's care, people, pastures, hills, meadows and valleys can sing together for joy (see Ps 65). God has sought always to feed us and gladden our hearts and to make the created world shine (see Ps 104).

The depth and richness of God's love are staggering and incomprehensible. Although we pull away and even try to de-create the world, God continually comes to us, recreating the world anew. Will we ever learn to be thankful for the love that does not let us go? It is time to take our humble and responsible place within God's abundant life, in which pain and death will be no more. This life, to which God invites us, begins here and now.

Acknowledgments

FRED BAHNSON:

The longer I try to live this life of discipleship, the more I realize just how indebted I am to friends. Along with my wife, it's my friends on whom I most often depend to teach me how to live. They've taught me to be a better father, husband, writer, gardener and moderate beer-drinker, especially how to pursue all those things for the glory of God. One of those friends is the coauthor of this book. It's been a joy to talk ideas with Norman over meals and beers, on his porch and mine. Other friends who bring me joy and keep me humble: Rob Bowers, Rich Church, Griff Gatewood, Tim Hammer, Baker Perry and Jeremy Troxler.

Given the onerous task of making a living as a writer, I have been fortunate enough to receive a number of generous writing grants, each coming at a crucial stage in my career and bestowing on me the best gift a writer can receive: time. For support during the writing of both this book and my forthcoming book *Soil and Sacrament* (Free Press), I'm grateful to Dorothy Bass, Don Richter and Susan Briehl at the Valparaiso Project on the Education and Formation of People in Faith, Mark Muller and Abby Rogosheske at the Institute for Agriculture and Trade Policy, and Don Richter (again) and Jim Lewis at the Louisville Institute.

For allowing me to descend upon them for three days, nibble on their plants and badger them with questions, I thank the good folks at ECHO, especially Stan and Beth Doerr, Martin Price, Tim Motis and Danielle Flood. Thanks to Julie Polter at *Sojourners*, who published an earlier version of the ECHO story in the August 2011 issue under the title "Ending the Hunger Season." For corresponding with me across oceans and sharing their good work, I thank Peter Cunningham and Claudio Oliver. For putting aside their own writing and reading various portions of mine, I'm grateful to Walter Brueggemann, Tom Lewis, Enuma Okoro and Ragan Sutterfield. For her encouragement and conversations on matters of land and faith, I thank Ellen Davis. Thanks to Jonathan Wilson-Hartgrove for his early enthusiasm about this book, and for helping it along.

For their love and support I thank my parents, my brother and sister, and the ever-growing Bahnson clan. Most of all, I give thanks for those with whom I share my life. Each is a bearer of God's image, each a singular gift: Elizabeth, Carsten, Elijah, David.

NORMAN WIRZBA:

Chris Rice and Emmanuel Katongole have spent too much time listening to me moan about how theological writing on reconciliation is anemic because it focuses only on human beings. They finally had the sense to say to me, "Write the book that will broaden and deepen our understanding of God's reconciling vision!" At long last, here it is.

Early on, Jonathan Wilson-Hartgrove saw the need for this book. His comments and suggestions for improvement have been gracious and right on target.

I could not have asked for a better coauthor for this project. Fred has been working with me on these matters for a long time. He understands my theological and philosophical abstractions and is able to show how they come to life in communities, gardens and fields all around the world. His insights and stories help me see where my theological reflection still needs to germinate and grow. His forthcoming book *Soil and Sacrament* will be a gift to the church.

I, along with Fred, thank Bill McKibben for his courageous work in defense of God's creation and for his willingness to write a foreword to this book. We also thank Judith Heyhoe for reading our manuscript and offering suggestions for improvement.

So many of my basic convictions took root while growing up in southern Alberta. Though I did not appreciate it then, I was blessed to work and worship with a generation of farmers who still subscribed to the ancient traditions of soil and animal husbandry. Foremost among these I must mention my grandfather Wilhelm Roepke. The way they cared for their farms and for each other, though hardly perfect, set an example for me of what peace with the land might look like.

The work of reconciliation, I believe, begins and is steadily nurtured by gratitude for the many gifts of God that sustain and make our life together a joy. I give thanks for my wife, Gretchen, and my children, Emily, Anna, Benjamin and Luke, each one a gift beyond all imagining or deserving.

Recommendations for Further Reading

THEOLOGICAL RESOURCES ON LAND, FOOD AND PEOPLE

Bahnson, Fred. *Soil and Sacrament: Four Seasons Among the Keepers of the Earth*. New York: Free Press, 2013.

Capon, Robert Farrar. *The Supper of the Lamb: A Culinary Reflection*. New York: Modern Library, 2002.

Davis, Ellen. *Scripture, Culture, and Agriculture: An Agrarian Reading of the Bible*. New York: Cambridge University Press, 2009.

Jung, L. Shannon. *Food for Life: The Spirituality and Ethics of Eating*. Minneapolis: Fortress, 2004.

Miles, Sara. *Take This Bread: A Radical Conversion*. New York: Ballantine, 2008.

Wirzba, Norman. *The Paradise of God: Renewing Religion in an Ecological Age*. New York: Oxford University Press, 2003.

———. *Food and Faith: A Theology of Eating*. New York: Cambridge University Press, 2011.

ENERGY, CLIMATE AND FOOD

Berry, Wendell. *The Art of the Commonplace*. Washington, D.C.: Counterpoint, 2012.

Jackson, Wes. *Consulting the Genius of the Place: An Ecological Approach to a New Agriculture.* Washington, D.C.: Counterpoint, 2010.

Kingsolver, Barbara. *Animal, Vegetable, Miracle: A Year of Food Life.* San Francisco: Harper, 2008.

Pollan, Michael. *The Omnivore's Dilemma: A Natural History of Four Meals.* New York: Penguin, 2007.

McKibben. Bill. *Deep Economies: The Wealth of Communities and the Durable Future.* New York: Times Books, 2008.

—————. *Eaarth: Making a Life on Tough New Planet.* New York: Times Books, 2010.

Worldwatch Institute. *State of the World 2011: Innovations that Nourish the Planet.* New York: W. W. Norton, 2011.

REGENERATIVE AGRICULTURE

Coleman, Eliot. *The New Organic Grower.* White River Junction, Vt.: Chelsea Green Publishers, 1995.

—————. *The Winter Harvest Handbook.* White River Junction, Vt.: Chelsea Green Publishers, 2009.

Hemenway, Toby. *Gaia's Garden: A Guide to Home-Scale Permaculture.* White River Junction, Vt.: Chelsea Green Publishing, 2009.

Jacke, Dave, and Eric Toensmeier. *Edible Forest Gardens.* 2 volumes. White River Junction, Vt.: Chelsea Green Publishing, 2005.

Jeavons, John. *How to Grow More Vegetables and Fruits.* New York: Ten Speed Press, 2006.

Logsdon, Gene. *The Contrary Farmer's Invitation to Gardening.* White River Junction, Vt.: Chelsea Green Publishing, 2008.

Price, Martin, and Laura Meitzner. *Amaranth to Zai Holes: Ideas for Growing Food Under Difficult Conditions.* North Fort Meyers, Fla.: ECHO Inc., 1996.

Reich, Lee. *Landscaping with Fruit.* North Adams, Mass.: Storey Publishing, 2009.

Study Guide

Questions for Personal Reflection or Group Discussion

Prologue

1. When you hear the word *creation,* what image comes to mind?

2. Do you find it helpful to think about God as Gardener? What other stories or images from Scripture come to mind as you read this account of Genesis?

3. The authors write, "God promised to never again destroy the world, but we humans just might." While we, as humans, recognize our capacity (and freedom) to destroy relationships, we often do not reflect on our capacity to destroy the planet. What questions does this knowledge raise for you? How does it challenge your understanding of providence and redemption?

4. What questions do you bring with you to this book? What issues do you hope to wrestle with while reading?

Chapter 1: Reconciliation with the Land

1. Norman writes, "Surely it is a contradiction to profess belief in the Creator while showing disregard or disdain for the works of the Creator's hands," yet he points out that this is, in fact, what most Christians do in practice. How does Norman account for this contradiction? Where do you see patterns of the "reconciliation deficit disorder" he describes in your own life?

2. Read the "Christ hymn" from Colossians 1:15-23. Spend some time thinking about the scope of Christ's reconciling work. What does the blood of Christ cover besides your own individual sins?

3. Norman describes the separation of body and spirit as a "Socratic urge." Why is this separation of the created order so tempting to Christians? How have you been tempted to practice this dualism in your own life? What does it look like to resist it in practice?

4. What does Norman mean by "ecological amnesia," and where does he say it comes from? What can we do to overcome it?

5. What difference does it make to approach an issue like mountain-top removal as a theological problem, rather than a political issue? Consider this statement:

   We did not come to this unprecedented state of affairs by people waking up each morning and plotting to destroy the earth. Instead, we have committed many small acts that we think will improve our standing in this world without realizing their disastrous ecological effects.

How might this perspective affect the way we talk about other social and ecological problems?

6. Why does God rest on the seventh day? How does sabbath help us understand what the creation is for?

Chapter 2: Learning to See

1. Fred offers a vivid image from the poet Scott Cairns of "animated earth." How does this way of imagining the "image of God" affect your own understanding of what it means to be a human being?

2. Fred insists that ecological concerns are not a "side issue," but rather, they sit right at the heart of what it means to be a Christian in our time. What are the implications of such a claim for the week-to-week life of a church community?

3. How does Fred's shift from mountain climbing to farming embody a resistance to the Socratic urge Norman described? What might someone who's not going to become a farmer take away from his story?

4. Fred argues that intimacy with God is closely linked with intimacy with the land. Have you experienced this in your own life? What spiritual deficits in our society do you see connected to our distance from the land?

5. What does it mean to "garden toward the *parousia*," rather than try to restore Eden? How might the humility Fred

is describing be embodied? Are there specific ways that drawing closer to the land could help you be more faithful in your own life and work?

Chapter 3: Reconciliation Through Christ

1. How does Norman see the abuse of land connected to the marginalization of people in Cedar Grove? Do you see similar dynamics where you live?

2. What does Norman mean when he says that Anathoth offers a "taste of heaven"? How does the biblical concept of *shalom* help us understand reconciliation that includes land?

3. Norman asks, "How do we know if our living . . . is truly good or rightly lived?" How does Jesus help him answer that question? How does Christology shape our imagination?

4. If "the ministry of reconciliation goes through a cross," what does that suggest we should expect from this world's systems? What does it teach us about the nature of Christian love?

5. Norman writes, "We need to develop practical forms of life that bring us into clarifying and sympathetic relationship with soil, plant and animal life." What might this look like where you live? What step could you take toward making it a reality this week?

Chapter 4: Field, Table, Communion

1. Fred makes a distinction between the abundance of God's kingdom and the "abundant mirage" of our present economy. What does this difference look like in daily living? What does it look like to fast from the abundant mirage? How can communities celebrate the abundance of God's kingdom?

2. What answers do you find most compelling and memorable to the question about what Christianity has to teach us about growing food? Why?

3. What practices help us remember that food is an "unearned gift from God"?

4. What might it look like to "consider the lilies" in the daily practices of our lives?

5. How do The Welcome Table and Casa da Videira embody the vision of justice and reconciliation that Fred and Norman are advocating? How does this story challenge the ways you or your church have engaged in mercy ministry?

6. Fred asks, "What if our homes and churches went from being primarily sites of *consumption* to places of *production*, as the scholar and priest Ivan Illich suggested?" Can you think of one way your household could produce something that you currently buy from a store? What would it look like to make this shift prayerfully, as an embrace of God's abundance?

Chapter 5: Reconciliation Through Eating

1. Norman writes, "God created a world in which every creature lives by eating." How do Jesus' teachings about and practice of eating help us to understand what it means to be part of the membership of creation?

2. Take a minute to think about how much you know about where the food you ate today came from. How do you feel about what you know? How do you feel about what you don't know? If we are ashamed of the food system we participate in, what do we do with that shame?

3. Have you been part of meals that "bore witness to God's continuing presence"? Try to name what it was that let you know Jesus was there.

4. Does it change your understanding of the Eucharist (or the Lord's Supper) to think of it as the "table where we go to die ourselves"? What might it mean for you to take this meal "out of the ritualistic realm" and make it a way of life?

5. Norman makes a distinction between self-offering and self-imposition. Can you think of a time when you engaged in self-imposition, even though you were trying to help or do good?

6. In the previous chapter, Fred wrote about opting out of the logic of our present system to experiment in the abundance of God's kingdom. In this chapter, Norman explores the need for a new farm bill and other structural changes to our world's food systems. How do we faithfully engage

a broken world with God's vision of reconciliation? What does God's vision of *shalom* and Jesus' way of the cross teach us about how to faithfully address a broken system?

Chapter 6: Bread for the Whole Body of Christ

1. How does ECHO embody a Christian witness in the midst of our world's present food crisis? Have you ever thought of farming as evangelism?

2. Antipoverty movements are often pitted against environmental movements, a concern for the poor versus a concern for the earth. How does the witness of ECHO show that making peace with creation means justice for all creatures?

3. What lessons does ECHO's witness offer for the big-picture issues of advocacy and systemic change? What challenges does it offer for day-to-day way of life issues?

4. Fred advocates for a kind of asset-based development that focuses not on the problem—namely, hunger—but on God's (and nature's) particular abundance. Where do you see that abundance in your community? How might you become a student of its ways and means?

Notes

page 43 "Then YHWH lay back": Scott Cairns, *Recovered Body,* George Braziller Publishers, 1998, reprinted by Eighth Day, 2003. Used by permission of the author.

pages 43-44 "The earth's sixth great species extinction event": www.guardian.co.uk/environment/2010/mar/07/extinction-species-evolve.

page 45 "Over the past 50 years": *Millennium Ecosystem Assessment,* www.maweb.org/en/Condition.aspx.

pages 45-46 "2010 tied with 2005": www.noaanews.noaa.gov/stories2011/20110112_globalstats.html.

page 46 "We're running Genesis backward": Bill McKibben, *Eaarth: Making a Life on a Tough New Planet* (New York: Times Books, 2010), p. 25.

page 48 "the backside of the calendar": Eliot Coleman, The Winter Harvest Handbook: Year-Round Vegetable Production Using Deep-Organic Techniques and Unheated Greenhouses (White River Junction, Vt.: Chelsea Green, 2009), introduction.

page 50 "a word not yet perceived": Bob Ekblad, *A New Christian Manifesto: Pledging Allegiance to the Kingdom of God* (Louisville, Ky.: Westminster John Knox, 2008), p. 86.

page 51 "agriculture is a ten-thousand-year-old bad habit": Wes Jackson, quoted from "Farmed Out: Wes Jackson on the Need to Reinvent Agriculture, interview with Fred Bahnson, *The Sun,* October 2010.

page 54   "Many American poets and novelists": Barry Lopez, *Home Ground: Language for an American Landscape,* ed. Barry Lopez and Debra Gwartney (San Antonio: Trinity University Press, 2006), p. xviii.

pages 55-56   "One must wait for the moment": Ibid.

page 57   "I think we are desperately in need": Marilynne Robinson, "Wilderness," *The Death of Adam* (New York: Houghton Mifflin, 1998), p. 253.

page 59   "Nothing can take the place of absolute contact": John Muir, quoted in David James Duncan and Rick Bass, *The Heart of the Monster* (Missoula, Mont.: All Against the Haul, 2010), introduction.

page 64   "My father, he gave land for a school": Audio and text available at http://wunc.org/programs/news/archive/anathoth_mp3.mp3/view.

page 79   "I have seen men share their bread": Quoted in Charles Marsh, *The Beloved Community: How Faith Shapes Social Justice, From the Civil Rights Movement to Today* (New York: Basic Books, 2004), p. 87.

page 81   "Fifteen years ago we went there": Ibid., p. 78.

page 83   One of my favorite stories: *The Sayings of the Desert Fathers,* translated by Benedicta Ward (Kalamazoo, Mich.: Cistercian Publications, 1975), p. 86.

page 87   "If you take it from the standpoint": Quoted in Lisa Hamilton, *Deeply Rooted: Unconventional Farmers in the Age of Agribusiness* (Berkeley, Calif.: Counterpoint, 2010).

page 89   "We know more than ever about the science of nutrition": http://colorlines.com/archives/2011/08/usda_guidelines_for_healthy_eating_too_costly_for_many_report_finds.html.

page 89   "Every culture has had": Raj Patel, *Stuffed and Starved: The Hidden Battle for the World Food System* (Brooklyn, N.Y.: Melville House, 2008), p. 3.

page 90 "nutrient content in commercially grown vegetables": Brian Halweil, *Still No Free Lunch: Nutrient Levels in U.S. Food Supply Eroded by Pursuit of High Yields,* The Organic Center report, www.organic-center.org/science .tocreports.html.

page 92 "The garden, like the kingdom of God": From author's conversation with Susan Sides, July 2011.

page 94 "When we pray that terrible prayer": Wendell Berry, remarks at Duke Divinity School convocation, October 2008.

page 94 "grounded in creation faith": Walter Brueggemann, unpublished paper, "The Food Fight," forthcoming in *Word & World.*

page 95 "what Liberty Hyde Bailey called *earth righteousness*": Liberty Hyde Bailey, *The Holy Earth: Toward a New Environmental Ethic,* introduction by Norman Wirzba (Dover, Del.: 2009), p. 18.

page 96 "contribute to the drawdown": Wes Jackson interview, *The Sun,* October 2010.

page 107 "consulting the genius": Wes Jackson, *Consulting the Genius of the Place: An Ecological Approach to New Agriculture,* (Washington, D.C.: Counterpoint, 2010).

page 107 "*Zoe* is what it's like to feel alive": From author's email exchange with Claudio Oliver, August 2011.

page 113 "who welcomes sinners and eats with them": See also Mt 9:11; Mk 2:16.

page 128 "When people, land, and community are as one": See www.land-institute.org/vnews/display.v/ART/2000 /08/10/37a747b43.

page 142 "Starvation is the characteristic of some people": Amartya Sen, *Poverty and Famines: An Essay on Entitlement and Deprivation* (New York: Oxford University Press, 1983), p. 1.

page 148   "an abundance that was almost certain": Raj Patel, *Stuffed and Starved: The Hidden Battle for the World Food System* (Brooklyn, N.Y.: Melville House, 2008).

page 148   "basically the use of industrial technology": Ibid.

About the
Duke Divinity School Center
for Reconciliation

Our Mandate

Established in 2005, the center's mission flows from the apostle Paul's affirmation in 2 Corinthians 5 that "God was in Christ reconciling the world to himself," and that "the message of reconciliation has been entrusted to us."

In many ways and for many reasons, the Christian community has not taken up this challenge. In conflicts and divisions ranging from brokenness in families, abandoned neighborhoods, urban violence and ethnic division in the United States to genocide in Rwanda and Sudan, the church typically has mirrored society rather than offering a witness to it. In response, the center seeks to form and strengthen transformative Christian leadership for reconciliation.

Our Mission

Rooted in a Christian vision of God's mission, the Center for Reconciliation advances God's mission of reconciliation in a divided world by cultivating new leaders, communicating wisdom and hope, and connecting in partnership to strengthen leadership.

Our Programs
- Serving U.S. leaders through an annual Summer Institute and Resources for Reconciliation book series
- Great Lakes Initiative in East Africa (Burundi, Congo, Kenya, Rwanda, South Sudan and Uganda) to nourish Christian leaders in the ministry of peace and reconciliation
- Annual Teaching Communities Week or Reconcilers Weekend featuring leading practitioners and theologians
- In-depth formation in the ministry of reconciliation through programs at Duke Divinity School
- Teaching Communities internships in exemplary communities of practice
- Visiting Practitioner Fellows

How You Can Participate
- Pray for us and our work.
- Partner financially with the center.
- *Join the journey.* Whether you are a student, pastor, practitioner, ministry leader or layperson, the center wants to support you in the journey of reconciliation. Explore our website and see how we might connect. www.dukereconciliation.com.

Please contact us for more information about the program to help support our work.

The Center for Reconciliation
Duke Divinity School
Box 90968
Durham, NC 27708
Phone: 919.660.3578
Email: reconciliation@div.duke.edu
Website: www.dukereconciliation.com

Resources for
Reconciliation

ABOUT RESOURCES FOR RECONCILIATION

Resources for Reconciliation pair leading theologians with on-the-ground practitioners to produce fresh literature to energize and sustain Christian life and mission in a broken and divided world. This series of brief books works in the intersection between theology and practice to help professionals, leaders and everyday Christians live as ambassadors of reconciliation.

Reconciling All Things
A Christian Vision for Justice,
Peace and Healing
Emmanuel Katongole and Chris Rice

Living Gently in a Violent World
The Prophetic Witness of Weakness
Stanley Hauerwas and Jean Vanier

Welcoming Justice
God's Movement Toward Beloved Community
Charles Marsh and John M. Perkins

Friendship at the Margins
Discovering Mutuality in Service and Mission
Christopher L. Heuertz
and Christine D. Pohl

Forgiving As We've Been Forgiven
Community Practices for Making Peace
L. Gregory Jones and Célestin Musekura

Living Without Enemies
Being Present in the Midst of Violence
Samuel Wells and Marcia A. Owen

Making Peace with the Land
God's Call to Reconcile with Creation
Fred Bahnson and Norman Wirzba